Transforming the
Transgenerational Trauma
of Your Family Tree

Step Into
The Light

Exploring Systemic Healing,
Inherited Emotional Genealogy,
Entanglements, Epigenetics and
Body Focused Systemic Constellations

Series Book 3

Patricia Kathleen Robertson

Step Into The Light

Transforming the Transgenerational Trauma of Your Family Tree

Exploring Systemic Healing, Inherited Emotional Genealogy, Entanglements, Epigenetics and

Body Focused Systemic Constellations

Series Book 3

Print ISBN: 978-1-54395-854-6

eBook ISBN: 978-1-54395-855-3

Front Cover: Painting "Rising Sun" by Patricia Robertson, February 5, 2017

Front Cover Design: Laurine Fillo Photography, Calgary, Alberta, Canada

Back Cover: Photo of Patricia by Laurine Fillo Photography, Calgary, Alberta, Canada

www.peacefulpossibilities.ca

Calgary, Alberta, Canada

I dedicate this book to all my teachers and mentors,
including my Earth Mother,
and all the wonderful creatures of the land, air and water;
to all the wonderful knowledgeable people
on every continent who have been willing to share,
for every scholar needs to find their teachers,
to begin the journey of learning, contemplation,
assimilation, integration and consolidation...

Family

The words in this book were written with much love
& deepest respect, honour, compassion
& gratitude to all my ancestors, who passed down
to me immense strength & resilience,
to my parents, James & Kay,
for giving me life, love, guidance
& always being there to support me,
to my siblings for sharing the journey,
& to my greatest teachers,
providing me with many profound life challenges,
Tristen, Nigel & Scott,
& the little ones that never came to life.

The soul, which is inclusive of all things,

is evident everywhere we look, when we look,

with the eyes of understanding and knowing.

I am reminded so often of the deeply moving moments

when clients have reverently bowed

to the fate of their ancestors,

feeling a deep sense of gratitude

that the ancestors' suffering

had led to the gift of their life

and its circumstances. [...]

These moments of grace are life-transforming.

To be witness to them has been my deepest honour,

for they stand testimony to the truth

that out of the deepest caverns of darkness

a bright light does shine.

- John L. Payne, *The Presence of the Soul:
Transforming Your Life Through Soul Awareness*

TABLE OF CONTENTS

INTRODUCTION

We are at an exciting turning point, and we are being asked energetically to step out of the darkness and into the light. The human spirit has been experiencing rapid technological change, and at the same time, an opening to deep emotional and spiritual advancement. This shift is global, and it pushes for inclusivity. We are being asked to change from a narrow, restrictive viewpoint to an all-encompassing and ever-expanding worldview. We are being asked to look at the big picture and to embrace a far greater perspective. We are being asked to develop our capacity for compassion, compassion for others, for Self and for the journey travelled by those who came before us. We are being asked to acknowledge and accept what is and what was, including the journey we have walked to get to the place where we are today. We are being asked to honour our journey as a vital part of our physical, mental, emotional, relational and spiritual advancement. That journey, regardless of how challenging it has been, has prepared each of us for what comes next. Transformation is not being presented as an option or a choice, but rather, it just is. We are being called to action, to embrace all that we are meant to be, by the greater collective energy field that surrounds us, flows through us and guides us on planet Earth. Change is here, and it is inevitable and swift. This change is much greater than you or I. We have the capacity to fathom only a small part of what is, and the rest is still a mystery. We are part of a much greater whole.

Willingness to Change

We flow more easily with any change when we accept that we are not in control. The best we can do is take responsibility for our own lives, remain present, and take charge of our responses and reactions. We are part of a plan that has been spiraling forward for millions of years. We can debate the human concept of free will until we are blue in the face, however, we really only have the choice as to how we decide to respond to this rapid change, how we respond to any change that confronts us. Millions of human beings are willingly following this rapidly changing path, opening to advancement with a deep sense of inner knowing and with a felt sense of resonance, others are anxiously observing from the sidelines with trepidation, while others are digging in their heels with great resistance and a defense of the status quo. Many are defending old institutions and old ways of being that no longer serve the wellbeing of the majority. It is a transformational time for all the institutions that have brought humankind to this moment - this point in time. Change is occurring within our traditional educational, legal, medical, psychological, political, organizational and religious institutions. The current systems are often not adequate to move us forward into this new era of heightened consciousness and higher vibrational being. We are frequently confounded by this rapid change, and to feel safe we let our ego rule our existence, loving the security found in what we know and what we have experienced in the past. Old habits and old neuronal pathways that developed in the brain to ensure evolutionary survival tend to create a resistance to change. We need to understand that many people living on the planet today are beyond basic survival, although this is a relatively new development. Many people have more time for reflection if they can silence the media overload. Evolution takes on new meaning today. You may find that you experience old thought patterns and old patterns of behaviour that repeat over and over. You may discover that these old habits and old pathways hold you back in life in some way. You may feel overwhelmed by the rapid pace of the change swirling around you or carry a feeling that life is passing you by.

We will thrive in this transformation, moving further forward into this new millennium when we embrace the change that is called for on the path we have chosen to take. Don't be surprised if fears arise. As well, you may feel sadness and mourning for what is being left behind. All of that is natural. They are normal human responses. Some of the change may include old friends stepping off your path and new ones appearing. I encourage you to open your heart at this immensely transformative time to experience all that is being made available to you in the 21st century. Each of us carries gifts within us, gifts of deep ancestral experience and wisdom, and gifts of knowing that aid our forward progress along this new expansive path. We are the descendants of the ancient wisdom keepers who came before us. This means we are the wisdom keepers of today. Our ancestors have been physical and psychological pioneers over the past few centuries and we are no different. We are the spiritual and emotional pioneers of today. Embrace that sensation.

The Flow of Time

The thread that trails through the past, present and future is becoming more obvious to us if we pause long enough to pay attention. We advance more rapidly when we let go of rigid attachment to linear time. Linear time means sensing time as a straight forward moving line. Linear time is a human construct, created for convenience, structure, security and a sense of control. To envision linear time, picture someone who has to punch a time clock when they arrive at work, punch the time clock for any break they take, and again punch the time clock when they leave the job site. Linear time creates a rigid sense of time. In reality, we belong to an expansive, multidimensional system of time and space, and at the moment it is beyond our current comprehension. However, that is slowly changing. We are being supported by time and space that spirals out in all directions beyond our own energy boundaries. Our interconnectedness to all that is, the great mystery and sacred Oneness, including the other creatures that share our planet, our environment, the air we breathe, the water that surrounds us and the unfathomable multiverse (more expansive than the concept of universe) within which we live, can no longer be ignored or arrogantly thought to be controllable. We are living the consequences of past arrogance. Mother Earth frequently rumbles with displeasure, lovingly flexing her immense power to bring us to a place of humility. Our potential and our capacity to reflect upon the past and learn from it, to shift the present and influence the future, are unprecedented.

Ancestral Wisdom

As I mentioned before, we are at a turning point or confluence, where we are beginning to value ancient wisdom that has been passed down orally from generation to generation. We are learning to value new approaches developed for transformation at a speed far beyond the slowly turning wheel of Darwin's evolution. We are being encouraged to embrace all those that walked upon Mother Earth ancestrally, within our own family system and out societally. It is a way to honour and respect the challenges of the past, and to honour the overwhelming obstacles to survival that were faced by our forebears. We begin to thrive when we acknowledge that each person did the best they could for their family system with the resources they had within them and around them. If you provide a silent space in your day, you can hear the ancestors whisper to you along the wind. Their vast life experiences, their triumphs and their challenges, are imprinted as collective memory deep within your bones and deep into the soil upon which you walk, and out into the collective energy field that surrounds you. You breathe the same air that they breathed, although it may not be as clean and fresh as it was in the past. That is something that we can change. We benefit when we are one with all those who walked before us. We bring the past, and all that we can learn from it, forward into the present, creating transformative potential for our children and grandchildren.

Step into the Light

Many people struggle to come out of the darkness and into the light. They intensely identify with their victimhood, anger, sadness, depression, resentment, guilt, relationship challenges or physical body symptoms. Their inner fear being, "Who am I without my victimhood?" "Who am I without my anger?" "Who am I without my guilt?" "Who am I without my symptoms?" It is evident that they fear the unknown, feeling greater safety with the status quo. The thought being along the lines of, "better the devil I know than the one I don't know." There is a fear of dropping the heavy façade that has developed overlaying their inner Self. They are afraid to find out what is left if that façade is dropped. Sometimes the action, *Step into the Light*, is misunderstood. Some people confuse it with going to the light at the end of the tunnel, a comment often heard after someone has a near death experience. If someone fears death, and that is a common fear, this leads to an unconscious fear of going over to the side of light and love, sensing that it may somehow put an end to their time on Earth, and they remain in the darkness or in the shadow rather than living life fully.

Systemic Healing Series

In this book, which is based on some of my past website blog posts on transgenerational trauma and systemic healing, with a huge amount of editing and added material of course, you will explore many topics that are controversial. As your worldview expands, you will find you are able to address subjects that once brought fear and a tendency to shut down or close emotionally. The chapters are presented in the order that they were originally written, so they may seem somewhat random. In combination with the other books of this Series, *Transforming the Transgenerational Trauma of Your Family Tree*, you will find a wide array of systemic healing topics explored and discussed. You will find that they are all interrelated in one way or another. You will explore several themes that have traditionally been relegated to the darkness, or silenced and labelled taboo, by family systems, institutions and societies, such as patriarchy, abortion and incest. These issues will be discussed in the context of transgenerational trauma and systemic healing. You will delve into the residential school systems that operated during colonization in many nations around the world in one form or another. They require you to look systemically at your family's relationship between the colonized and the colonizer, and the Indigenous and the non-Indigenous. It is time to expose all of these topics to the light. As you commit to exploring these themes, you evolve systemically and emotionally, aligning with the greater shifting movement of human-ity. Like the many topics reviewed in Book 1 of this series, *Connect With Your Ancestors*, or Book 2, *Let Your Tears Flow*, each theme becomes less controversial when it reaches the light, bringing awareness, expansion and energetic wellbeing. All of these topics are explored through relationships, considered key aspects of human development. You will look at the importance of having a healthy porous energy boundary in life to create healthy relationships with the living and the dead, and you will explore the value of having a healthy relationship with Self. This book addresses the issues that flow transgenerationally between mothers and daughters, as the bearers of children and the most significant emotional caregivers of the next generations, and it looks at what can be done to create healthy relationships that don't burden the next generation.

What's a Constellation?

You will notice in this book that there are many references to systemic and family constellations, a phenomenological and multidimensional way to map out life challenges and concerns right before your eyes. Constellations can bring forward new insight, a whole new perspective or a new image for understanding and moving forward with a person's life issues, concerns or challenges. Constellation work can be done in a large circle with many people participating, in small groups or one to one with the facilitator and the client. It can also be done online using Skype or other online video conferencing services. In a workshop situation, the facilitator will ask the greater circle of participants, "who would like to do some work or look at an issue?" The person who responds becomes the client. The client sits down in the circle beside the facilitator. The facilitator often asks the client to briefly describe the issue they want to address and then asks a few more questions to get a sense of the client's issue and perhaps the dynamics of the client's family system. The facilitator may tune into their own body and also into the body of the client to get an energetic feel for the concern or the energy dynamics surrounding the issue. The facilitator guides the client's systemic emotional healing work throughout the constellation, continually monitoring their wellbeing. The facilitator usually decides what representatives are needed to set up the issue. It is often good to start with a small number of representatives. Representatives can be people, places, countries, land, objects, emotions, options or any other abstract energy such as love, light or the client's highest good. The live representatives might be asked to represent the client's mother or father or sibling or maternal grandmother to look at a family situation. As well, there is often a representative set up for the client themselves. In other types of constellations, a representative might be set up for the client and one for their symptom to look at a chronic condition. Either the client or the facilitator selects the representatives from the larger circle to represent the different aspects of the client's issue. In a workshop, these live representatives are set out in the inner work space of the circle to show the relationship between people or issues, or to show emotional direction or distance from one another.

There are many ways to set up a constellation depending on the issue presented. In one to one work, markers, which might be paper, felt or ornamental, are used to represent the different aspects of the client's family or issue. When using live representatives, the client may be asked to position the representatives within the circle, or sometimes the representatives are asked by the facilitator to find their own place in the space available. As the constellation begins, the representatives are asked to feel into their body to sense the energy of what or who they are representing. Representatives may begin to feel angry or sad, or they may feel that they want to turn away or move further away from one of the other representatives. Many different responses are possible. The facilitator checks in with the various representatives and asks them what is going on for them. In turn, the representatives respond to the facilitator. The constellation continues to evolve as representatives reveal new aspects about the family, organization or nature system, as they are felt in the body of the representative or as they pop into the mind of the representative seemly out of nowhere. Whether simple markers or live representatives are used in the constellation, they seem to take on the energy of the client's actual family members and ancestors. This is one of the more mysterious, phenomenological aspects of the work. The greater energetic collective field surrounding the constellation work is known as The Knowing Field.

Emotional healing work is done with the client as they observe, recognize, acknowledge and accept what is revealed in a constellation at a deep emotional body level. The facilitator continually checks in with the client to see if they are in resonance with the constellation or if they are struggling to take in the image presented in front of them. The facilitator monitors the client's response to what is being revealed. A systemic or family constellation resembles the star constellations of the night sky, with each representative positioned like a star in a constellation, only a systemic constellation continues to shift and move before your eyes. The stars in the night sky are moving and shifting too, however, they move at a speed that is not visible to the naked eye because of the great distance between them and us. This is only a very brief description of a systemic or family constellation. There are many books written about systemic and family constellations and I encourage you to review the list of suggested readings at the end of this book if you are interested in learning more about this approach to wellbeing, or alternatively, book a session with a facilitator.

The Purpose of This Book

My purpose is to discuss many of the topics that arise in systemic and family constellations from a transgenerational trauma and systemic healing point of view. As we learn to look systemically at our challenges in life, we realize that events and people of the past continue to show up in our lives in the present, and not necessarily in a physical state. You may be surprised to learn that in every family there is a collection of transgenerational trauma that may tie into any number of these topics. Sometimes it takes your acknowledgement that these past events, situations and people had some relevancy for your ancestors, connecting them to your family system, your current life and the lives of your children and grandchildren. Sometimes it takes a deeper look at both the light and shadow side of your life and that of your family system. Sometimes we need to admit that we carry the energy of both the victim and the perpetrator, since our ancestors did what they had to do for their own survival and the survival of their family systems.

What's Included?

As a quick reminder, Book 1 of this Series, *Connect With Your Ancestors*, systemically and transgenerationally explored topics such as radical inclusion; belonging or fitting into the family system; what to do if you feel stuck in life; emotional wounds and entanglements; relationships with father; emotional wounds of men; give and take in relationships; how to stop living in agency; how to look systemically at symptoms, conditions and repetitive behaviours; and the transformational healing role of ritual in our lives. Book 2, *Let Your Tears Flow*, addressed some fascinating systemic topics to guide you toward living life fully, such as what it means to be drawn to the dead, the transgenerational trauma of immigration, relationships for adopted children, the lingering sensations felt in the body with the death of a twin, common family transgenerational dynamics, epigenetics, systemic relationships with former partners, the systemic impact of separation on children and the systemic dynamics when a child is born to a woman in mourning. Many of these themes seem specific in nature, however, there is a little for everyone in each topic.

Dear reader, you may be immediately drawn to read some chapters before others and I encourage you to do so. The chapters can be read in any order without losing any sense of the book, unless they have Part 1, Part 2 and Part 3, and then I suggest you read them in order. I also encourage you to read the chapters that don't draw your attention. Sometimes there is an unconscious or transgenerational reason why a person avoids certain subjects, and deep meaning may be found within them when you openly embrace these topics. Sometimes your family system or your society silenced these themes. It is my objective to provide information on new systemic ways to broach the challenging topics of life. This is my interpretation – one amongst many. I encourage you to challenge what I have written and to sort out your own feelings or belief system about each theme. Figure out whether your belief system is serving you well or whether it is leaving you feeling stuck in life. Sort out whether your belief system flows from a place of fear and exclusion, or a place of love and inclusion. Leave behind what others have told you throughout life and sense what feels right inside you. While some topics may seem irrelevant to your own family system, let yourself wander to the challenges faced by other family members, friends, neighbours, colleagues and coworkers. We all learn from the examples shared by others. We all learn through the lives of others. Delve into this discussion of transgenerational trauma and systemic healing, looking for the patterns that stand out from amongst the conflict and chaos, finding the threads that connect one situation or person to another, and grasping onto the links that seem relevant. I hope the comments I offer provide significant meaning in your life. This is an opportunity to gain some new insight or a fresh perspective about the challenges of your family system. I encourage you to look back at people, events and situations without blame or judgement. Find compassion for all those who travelled before you, bringing you to this magnificent turning point on planet Earth. It is when we feel gratitude for life itself that we can *Step into the Light* with anticipation, joy and delight.

AUGUST

Residential Schools

Written August 17, 2014

There has been one more death far too soon, and one death is too many. This chapter was written with respect for the Indigenous Peoples of Canada and the First Peoples of other nations around the world. Many are continuing to experience transgenerational emotional trauma, individually, within families and within communities today as a result of long-term destructive government legislation and residential school systems meant to assimilate populations and destroy Indigenous cultures during the process of colonization. The emotional legacies of the Canadian and American residential school systems are long and transgenerational. It was a system that helped to inspire the destruction caused by Apartheid in South Africa. Cultural genocide was the intent. Many people still living today attended the residential schools, or alternatively, the day schools. This is not ancient history and we cannot ignore it like it is. There are those living today who did not attend the schools personally, many of them descendants, yet they inherited and experience the emotional transgenerational trauma of the residential schools affecting their lives. It is time to address this insidious emotional inheritance that creates devastating outcomes for First Peoples in many aspects of their daily lives.

Residential School Resource Material

Resources describing the residential school experience and impact in Canada may be found through the research series of the Aboriginal Healing Foundation of Canada[1], the archives of the Truth and Reconciliation Commission of Canada in Winnipeg[2] or feel free to download my major research paper, a requirement for my Master of Arts in Conflict Analysis and Management completed in 2011 through Royal Roads University in

---

1 Research was completed on many themes related to the residential schools within the Aboriginal Healing Foundation of Canada, www.ahf.ca/publications/research-series
2 Truth and Reconciliation Commission of Canada, www.trc.ca

Victoria, British Columbia.[3] The most important part of the research paper is the survey results, which are the opinions of Indigenous and non-Indigenous individuals with long histories of bringing together peoples of different cultures in Canada. They were adamant that personal healing is imperative and that it is a lifelong journey. There is no magic solution. Healing a whole nation occurs one individual at a time. The band-aid has now been ripped off and the wound is wide open thanks to the work of the Truth and Reconciliation Commission of Canada from 2010 to 2015 and many other committed individuals and organizations. We all benefit when the silence is lifted and an issue of great concern is brought into the light. Systemic healing now calls for your attention to initiate healing in your own life and within your own family system. Systemic healing is needed whether you are Indigenous to the land you live upon, or whether you are a Settler, a member of a family that immigrated to the land you live upon, and regardless of whether immigration occurred last week or four hundred years ago. The wound is no longer hidden from view, yet it continues to dangerously fester.

Systemic Impact

The immediate emotional, cultural and environmental impact of the Indian Residential School System (IRSS) and other assimilative and discriminatory Canadian legislation such as the Gradual Civilization Act of 1857, the Gradual Enfranchisement Act of 1869, the Indian Act of 1876[4],

---

3 Robertson, P. (2011). *Healing the personal wounds of colonization: Utilizing third party consultation to transform Canada's post-residential school societal conflict.* Major Research Paper Royal Roads University. The research paper can be found at ResearchGate or at academia.edu using the following link: www.academia.edu/7208215/Healing_the_personal_wounds_of_colonization_Utilizing_third_party_consultation_to_transform_Canadas_post-residential_school_societal_conflict.
4 Robinson, A. (2016). Gradual Civilization Act. *Historica Canada.* Retrieved February 2018 from http://www.thecanadianencyclopedia.ca/en/article/gradual-civilization-act/

the Vagrancy Act 1889[5], The White Paper 1969[6] and Bill C-31[7] in 1985, to name a few, was systemic and greatly impactful across hundreds of communities and tribal groups. The emotional trauma created by these experiences and legislation was imprinted deeply into the cells of the bodies of everyone involved. Anything I have written in the past about victims, perpetrators and radical inclusion is important here. This legislation was intentionally exclusionary. Anything that is exclusionary creates a systemic wound, and systemic wounding tends to find healing systemically. What multiple generations of parents and grandparents felt emotionally and suppressed as a result of the residential school experience, and what the current living generations feel emotionally and are suppressing, is flowing epigenetically and unconsciously downward to the children, grandchildren, great grandchildren and future generations. This impact stretches beyond seven generations and it may take many generations to generate overall adequate to thriving levels of wellbeing. It will take a critical mass within non-Indigenous society, since that constitutes about ninety-five percent of the population in Canada, to shift limiting mindsets present today. It is the responsibility of each living member of society to make an intentional conscious decision to end the destructive transgenerational emotional legacy of these residential schools. This is relevant throughout the world today.

Let me draw from the work of Deborah Chansonneuve[8], as she succinctly revealed some of the impacts of residential schools at the individual level:

- There is widespread loss of culture, language, spirituality, pride in culture, family nurturing, and feelings of confidence and self-esteem;

- There are feelings of humiliation, shame, abandonment and guilt;

5 Moss, W. & Gardner-O'Toole, E. (1987/1991). *Aboriginal People: History of Discriminatory Laws BP-175E*. Retrieved February 19, 2018 from http://publications.gc.ca/Collection-R/LoPBdP/BP/bp175-e.htm

6 First Nations & Indigenous Studies: The University of British Columbia. (2009). *The White Paper 1969*. Retrieved February 19, 2018 from http://indigenousfoundations.web.arts.ubc.ca/the_white_paper_1969/

7 First Nations & Indigenous Studies: The University of British Columbia. (2009). *Bill C-31*. Indigenousfoundations.arts.ubc.ca. Retrieved February 19, 2018 from http://indigenousfoundations.web.arts.ubc.ca/bill_c-31/

8 Chansonneuve, D. (2005). Reclaiming connections: Understanding residential school trauma among Indigenous People. Ottawa: ON: Aboriginal Healing Foundation (pp. 46-47).

- There is a devaluation of women; and,

- There are communication barriers and an inability to express affection.

Chansonneuve continued her list with the impacts of residential schools at the family level:

- There has frequently been a lack of family affection for generations and patterns of traumatic bonding, inconsistent or extreme expressions of love and an inability to show affection through hugs;

- There is a lack of communication in the family and a loss of bonding between siblings;

- Many children are taken from homes by child services;

- Many people carry deep feelings of remorse;

- There is silence and shame from abuse repeated in the home;

- Gifts and material things are used to soothe wounds in the family;

- Information about Indian Residential School experiences is not passed to children because of the abuse experienced, and fear of retraumatizing; and,

- Emotional abuse and lateral violence are common, accompanied by anger, jealousy, resentment and/or gossip at or against one other.

Chansonneuve added the impacts of residential schools on whole communities:

- There are high rates of family violence, suicide ideation and suicide;

- Many people lack traditional skills and live without role models;

- Many communities are overwhelmed by unhealthy living conditions and overcrowding;

- Addictive and self-destructive behaviours are common, including substance abuse, sexual abuse, sex trade activity and gambling;

- There are ongoing power and control issues;

- There is often an inability to face community abuse and dysfunction, and many people feel isolated within the community;

- Racism, racial scaling and legislation that uses blood quantum are exclusionary;

- Many communities experience a lack of self-sufficiency and sustainability;

- Problems that exist on reserves follow those who migrate to urban communities;

- While many people have a strong desire to reclaim traditional cultural and spiritual identity, they have to contend with spiritual and religious splits within family systems and within the community; and,

- It is common for community members to come together during crises, but they cannot sustain this cooperation with positive energy at other times.

Chansonneuve (2005) was adamant that many individuals, families and communities struggle with multiple items on this extensive list of issues.

The History

Indigenous children as young as four or five years old were forcibly torn from the hands of their parents and grandparents and sent to schools, frequently great distances from the family home and community. These actions were legislated and enforced by the Government of Canada from the mid 1800s to the 1990s. The parents had no choice but to give up their children to the system. When the children were gone, the life force energy of the community was gone. For many left behind, their whole purpose for living, the reason for being parents and grandparents was gone. Intergenerational organization of communities was severely disrupted. Understanding self-identity and self-motivation tended to vanish. Within the communities, early addictive behaviours ensued with substances generally supplied by the colonizers. Addictions were used to numb the pain or escape the emptiness felt within the body, the mind, the heart and the spirit. Grandparents no longer had anyone to receive their love, care, culture and stories. Many parents lost their capacity to parent effectively without their children present. Parenting is a learned skill developed through experience. In many families, there were no longer any children to parent. There was a void that could not be filled in families and communities.

In the schools, the children experienced: alienation; loneliness; fear; separation from siblings, friends and family; an aggressive assault on identity; foreign ways and foods; violence; abuse; spiritual annihilation; cultural annihilation; disease; and death. Some managed to have kind caregivers and the impact was less severe. However, cultural genocide was the intention[9] and that cannot be denied even if some children emerged more resilient than others. All Canadians were directly or indirectly involved and impacted by the implementation of cultural genocide on the First Peoples, and this impact is felt heavily by collective society today.

Let me provide the legal definition of genocide from the Office of the United Nations Special Adviser on the Prevention of Genocide (OSAPG)[10]:

"Genocide is defined in Article 2 of the Convention on the Prevention and Punishment of the Crime of Genocide (1948) as 'any of the following acts committed with intent to destroy, in whole or in part, a national, ethnical, racial or religious group, as such: killing members of the group; causing serious bodily or mental harm to members of the group; deliberately inflicting on the group conditions of life

---

9 Robertson, P. (2018/2016). *Measuring the Quantitative Transgenerational Trauma Impact of Cultural Genocide in Canada on Métis, Inuit and First Nations Peoples Living Off Reserve Today Resulting from Past Generations of Family Members Attending Residential School.* Quantitative Research Paper Royal Roads University. The research paper can be found at academia.edu using the following link: *https:// www.academia.edu/35743107/Measuring_the_Quantitative_Transgenerational_Trauma_Impact_ of_Cultural_Genocide_in_Canada_on_M%C3%A9tis_Inuit_and_First_Nations_Peoples_Living_ Off_Reserve_Today_Resulting_from_Past_Generations_of_Family_Members_Attending_Residential_School*
10 Legal Definition of Genocide (1948). United Nations: Office of the UN Special Adviser on the prevention of Genocide (OSAPG): Analysis Framework. Retrieved from www.un.org/en/prevent-genocide/adviser/pdf/osapg_analysis_framework.pdf

calculated to bring about its physical destruction in whole or in part; imposing measures intended to prevent births within the group; [and] forcibly transferring children of the group to another group.'"

Article 2 describes exactly what the Canadian Federal Government imposed on the First Peoples.

The Experience of the Young Child

To give an example of the intensity of fear that was experienced by a young child, picture the following: You are raised in the northern territories of Canada and one day a large, rather strange looking, bird-like contraption soars through the air and then it lands on the water of the lake near your home. It glides ominously along the surface of the water toward your settlement. Some strange looking people with pasty pale skin, hairy faces and strange clothing get out of the contraption and beckon to your parents. Your parents are told that you, your brother and your sisters must climb inside the flying contraption and go live at a school a thousand miles away to the south. They are told that an education is good for their children. You have no idea what a thousand miles means. There is no option. There is no time. Your parents are told that you must climb into the flying machine now. You must go to school or else your parents will be punished by the new government of the land. Slowly… your mother packs a small hide bag with clothing and possessions for you, your brother and your two sisters. She has made all of your possessions herself with great love. She tucks in a beautiful feather to help you remember her. Tears run down her cheeks. Your parents give each of you a big hug and then you are lead away by this stranger toward the flying machine. Your mother and father are weeping, and they are calling out to you to be strong. They are telling you that you will see one another again soon. Feeling great fear rise within your body, you reluctantly do as you are told. You tremble uncontrollably as you step toward the strange bird. You, your little brother and your two older sisters hold hands as you step toward the monstrous bird. You are afraid of being swallowed up. You close your eyes as you step inside. After a moment, you open your eyes and realize you are still alive. Your heart is pounding. You feel your body shake with fear as this great bird begins to rumble and roar. You have never been anywhere without your mother and father. You have never left your settlement except to go out on the water or ice to help your father fish or out on the land to trap an animal for food. As the bird takes to the air, you look back at your mother and father and they look so small and sad.

When you arrive at the school more strangers take away all your possessions from home and you never see them again. They discard the beautiful feather given to you by your mother. They shave off your long dark braids of hair. They strip off your clothing and hose you down with cold water in front of many strangers and cover you in a cloud of dusty powder. They put you in strange clothing and feed you strange food. They punish you when you are caught speaking your mother tongue. You rarely get to see or speak to your brother or sisters. You don't realize it at the time, but the next time you will see your mother, father and your home again is eight long years away. By then your beloved grandparents will no longer be living. You will have a great amount of emotional pain suppressed inside your body from all that you have experienced. When you arrive home once again and look upon the faces of the loving parents you left behind, you will barely recognize them, and the meeting will feel very awkward. You will need to dig deeply into the recesses of your memory and deep within your heart and what is left of your spirit to connect with that thread of love... that thread that you know has kept you alive these many long years. You feel a tug at your heart string with the joy you feel at reconnecting with your parents, and yet, it is somehow covered over with sadness for the time that has passed ... for your mother and father look so much older than the way you remember them. You no longer speak the language of your community and you struggle to communicate with the few words that come to mind. You and your siblings feel like total strangers within your own family and community. Valuable time has passed that cannot be reclaimed... for it is lost forever...

Family

Legacy of Canada's Indian Residential Schools

Written August 24, 2014

The systemic impact of colonization influences the lives of people all over the world today, impacting the wellbeing of individuals, families and communities. In Canada or the United States, having knowledge of the legacy of the Indian Residential Schools and other assimilative legislation and practices is vital to understanding the social, cultural, economic and political reality and dynamics today for Indigenous Peoples. Within this chapter I will focus on the systemic impact of residential schools in Canada. Non-Indigenous Canadians, known as the Immigrants or Settlers, need to open their hearts and minds to learn some semblance of an accurate history of the land, and gain an understanding of how the past is influencing the present. I encourage you not to rely on old history books for this information, and sometimes current history books are still not accurate by omission. The Canadian Truth and Reconciliation Commission is a good source for this history. Non-Indigenous Canadians generally go about life with little knowledge and understanding of the ongoing devastating effect of the Indian Residential Schools on Indigenous Peoples. About 150,000 Indigenous children were forced away from their families to attend residential schools from the mid 1800s until 1996. This profoundly impacted the wellbeing of numerous generations in many families. Today, there is a detrimental disconnection between the cause and the effect. People may hear about the struggles of individuals and families within Indigenous communities in the news today, but rarely do they pause to draw a link from the struggles they learn about to the residential schools and destructive assimilative legislature for almost two centuries as the key underlying reasons for the hardships that are endured by Indigenous Peoples today. This is not something that the First Peoples can "just get over." Disconnection is the transgenerational trauma legacy of Canada's Indian Residential Schools for both the First Peoples and the Settlers.

Frequently, any fleeting recognition is filed away deeply into the unconscious mind as an emotional protective mechanism, and conscious acknowledgement is not generated. It has the effect of burying your head in the sand. Some people might have the brief thought that the government has to deal with that issue - it's not my issue. An unfortunate result of this "head in the sand" approach is that new Canadians are often even more intolerant of the legacy of Canada's Indian Residential Schools because they are usually passed misinformation from other members of non-Indigenous society. As mentioned in the last chapter, Settler families make up about ninety-five percent of Canadians. This includes all immigrants and refugees to Canada regardless of whether immigration occurred centuries ago or yesterday. The reality is that new immigrants or refugees to the land bring the transgenerational trauma of their ancestral homeland with them and they inherit the transgenerational trauma of their new land. It is the same dynamic as moving into a new family through marriage or co-habitation. You bring the transgenerational trauma of your own family system with you and you inherit the transgenerational trauma of the family you join. That is the systemic impact of immigration. It takes intentional action by this ninety-five percent to change the system for the five percent with Indigenous ancestry. First Nations, Inuit and Métis live with transgenerational trauma in many of their families and communities as a result of at least one hundred and fifty years of Canadian government policy encouraging dependency through the Indian Act and other destructive legislative policies; and enforcing assimilation and cultural genocide through its tool - the Indian Residential Schools. That is our history, the legacy of Canada's Indian Residential Schools, and healing can begin when the majority or a critical mass take responsibility. Step one is learning the history, not as it was taught from the history books for decades through the eyes of the colonizers, but through the eyes of those who lost so much.

Reality Revealed

When did the discussion on the residential schools finally begin? Many residential school survivors kept their painful emotional experiences suppressed and buried in the cells of their bodies for decades. It was a silence similar to the decades that followed the destruction of the Holocaust after World War II. Many took their pain to their graves. Most did not share their experiences with family or friends. For others, the pressure to remain silent became impossible and they finally began to speak about their experiences publicly in the late 1980s. Between 2010 and 2015, thousands shared their experiences of the residential schools with the Canadian Truth and Reconciliation Commission statement gatherers, while others shared their experiences earlier during the Settlement Agreement process. Some have written books. The truth is slowly trickling out. A great number of the Indigenous children who attended Canada's federally funded, mostly mainline church operated, Indian Residential Schools were the victims of physical, sexual, psychological and cultural abuse during their years at the schools. Most children struggled under the oppression. Many others went missing. Many children died without proper notification to the family about the cause of death, and proper burials were frequently non-existent.

In addition to the intentional destruction of the Indigenous Peoples' cultural identity; language; traditions; ceremonies; intergenerational skills such as parenting and survival skills; and spiritual beliefs, songs and dances; many children also left the schools carrying terrible shame and guilt imposed on them by adults in positions of trust. Additionally, many children were not openly welcomed home when they returned to their communities. Family and community ties seemed to be irreparably damaged. Many lost any sense of belonging. Many children were stuck between cultures. Many administrators, supervisors, government agents, teachers, clergy, support staff and church workers forced abuses on the children. Older oppressed and abused Indigenous students were forced to abuse younger children. It wasn't enough just to tear these children away from their families at four or five years of age, but school treatment included:

violence, constant fear tactics, inappropriate discipline, hunger, degradation, cruelty, forbidden use of mother tongues under threat of punishment, isolation from siblings, forced labour, the loss of cultural and spiritual traditions, a sudden and complete diet change, the loss of valued mementos from parents and grandparents, and a sterile, institutional atmosphere to replace loving family and community members. For the parents and grandparents, the abrupt loss of their children and grandchildren from the family unit and community was devastating. Would you want this for your children and grandchildren? If you are a non-Indigenous person living in Canada today, you can stop wondering why so many Indigenous Peoples are still struggling. This is not something that you can just get over without deep body focused emotional and spiritual systemic healing. This unresolved emotional trauma travels transgenerationally down from one generation to the next. Addressing transgenerational trauma requires a systemic body focused healing approach. As I edit this chapter, another baby of Indigenous ancestry has already been born carrying this transgenerational trauma emotional inheritance.

Assimilation

Indigenous communities are living with the legacy of destructive Canadian legislation. The intent was cultural destruction. The Indian Residential Schools were implemented with genocidal purpose in the United States and Canada to kill the Indian in the child, or "kill the Indian and save the man"[11] to "civilize" and Christianize. It is only fair to note that many people complicit in this process thought they were involved to "better" the Indigenous Peoples. That doesn't make any of it right. There was an underlying attitude of superiority under all the actions and behaviours. There was no respect shown for the Indigenous way of life for thousands of years. I must also emphasize that not all residential school experiences were considered negative and some people feel their time at the schools

---

11 Full text of Capt. Richard H. Pratt's "Kill the Indian, and Save the Man" speech, 1892, central to the development of the Carlisle Indian School (founded 1879) in the USA. History Matters, George Mason University.http://carlisleindian.dickinson.edu/teach/kill-indian-and-save-man-capt-richard-h-pratt-education-native-americans

gave them a positive boost in life. However, many of these individuals have suppressed the negative and destructive aspects of the schools, including the cultural genocide, to move forward. They have drawn on their cultural resilience and they are survivors. Each individual makes a choice as to how they move forward. Stoicism doesn't resolve the emotional trauma they store deep within themselves. The reality is that unresolved emotional trauma experienced by those living in the past, or those still living today, has already been passed down to their children, grandchildren and great grandchildren. The suppressed trauma manifests as physical, emotional, spiritual, psychological, mental, intellectual, financial and relational symptoms and conditions. This unresolved emotional trauma needs to be addressed one person at a time because their experiences were highly contextual.

One generation may succeed in moving forward without the healing work being done, however, in all likelihood, their children and grandchildren will exhibit the unresolved emotional trauma of the past in their lives, sometimes in a more powerful way, highlighting the need for healing to occur. Any emotional trauma experienced shifts the expression of the genes, epigenetically, from one generation to the next. Emotional, physical, mental, spiritual, psychological and relational woundedness does not occur in isolation and systemic healing does not occur in isolation. There is a greater collective system, beyond the individual, that calls for healing, wellness and balance. Silence and avoidance may only perpetrate greater transgenerational unwellness. Repetitive life patterns lived by the mother, father and grandparents may occur in the new generations, over and over, until the deep emotional healing work is done. Each successive generation feels the transgenerational trauma more profoundly when it is not worked through emotionally and systemically by the prior generations.

It's Your History and Mine

Discussing any positive aspects of the residential schools does not right thousands of wrongs or abusive situations. Our parents and ancestors were human beings and as such they made many mistakes. That is something we all need to own. We look back without blame and judgement to honour their humanity. This was a shameful period in Canadian history and in other nations around the world such as the United States and Australia. Through my own systemic healing work, and through systemic and family constellations, I have learned to acknowledge and accept the past for what it was and is. It was what it was. We cannot change the past. It does not resolve anything to carry the negative emotions of anger, shame, guilt, pain, trauma, resentment or hatred forward with us. These emotions only keep a person stuck, paralyzed emotionally, and unable to live out their full potential. I am referring to both Indigenous and non-Indigenous Peoples here. Addressing the emotional wounds through systemic body focused approaches brings healing. We cannot change the past, however, looking to the past is essential. In the present, we can acknowledge the past and learn from it. If we don't take the time to learn from the past we may continue the same repetitive patterns in one form or another. We continue to witness more of this oppressive behaviour and action all over the world today, including ongoing oppression within Canada. Canadian colonization of Indigenous Peoples continues today. Governments cannot seem to put together healthy new legislation in collaboration with First Peoples. With a short-term outlook, fed by a desire for re-election, politicians and government employees are remiss in not building sustainable, strong and healthy relationships with Indigenous Peoples, their leadership and their communities. Over and over new legislation is overturned by Indigenous Peoples because the papers put forward are still destructive. Legislation developed over the past few decades has tended to explicitly or implicitly eliminate or reduce the rights of First Peoples. Governments need to involve Indigenous Peoples, and not just in a token way, in the development of legislation that will impact their lives. Collaboration cannot be an afterthought.

National or provincial history passes down from generation to generation just as family and community history does. The nation has a collective consciousness that is greater than the sum of its parts. This collective is bigger than all of us. The tragedies and traumas left unresolved from the past, within the nation and on the land upon which we all live, may flow down energetically to the next generations until they are resolved or healed systemically. What arrives with the immigrants, whether recent or long ago in the past, the trauma imprinted deep within the cells of their bodies, also needs to be addressed. The people in power within Canadian governments at all levels do not easily recognize the Indigenous Peoples as nations and they don't readily accept their right to self-determination. They plead ignorance when evaluating the true intentions behind the many Treaties signed with First Peoples. They act as if their forebears signed real estate deals with the First Peoples, handing over all their territorial land. They avoid looking at the deep trauma caused and refuse to take honest, respectful responsibility for the pain caused. The First Peoples are frequently looked upon as a problem rather than as stakeholders in a strong Canadian wellness solution moving forward.

Healing the Wounds

Just as a family heals when it welcomes in those who are missing, forgotten, or excluded; so too does a nation heal its wounds when those who are excluded, shunned or pushed to the margins of society find themselves openly welcomed and included. This welcome will be noticeable when those who were formerly marginalized have the opportunity to live a similar average standard and quality of life with those of dominant society. Canada has a lo-o-o-ooong way to go! Canada usually ranks in the top six or seven placements on the United Nations Human Development Index each year for standard of living. However, the Indigenous Peoples living in Canada are often ranked around 50th worldwide.[12] This latter statistic needs to shift dramatically, not as an option but as an imperative!

What we learn from the past can be used to change the future, if we are open, ready and willing to change. What we learn from the past

---

12 Anaya, J. (July 4, 2014). Retrieve from http://unsr.jamesanaya.org/docs/countries/2014-report-canada-a-hrc-27-52-add-2-en.pdf. James Anaya holds the position of United Nations Special Rapporteur on the rights of indigenous peoples in Canada.

can be used for healing systemically at the individual, family, community, regional, national and global levels. The Chair of the Canadian Truth and Reconciliation Commission declared, "reconciliation is about forging and maintaining respectful relationships. There are no shortcuts."[13] People are often given the impression that the Indian Residential Schools (IRS) are part of Canada's long ago distant history, but that is misinformation. The last residential school closed at Gordon in the province of Saskatchewan in 1996. I find the following quote so appropriate and it comes from Kath Walker (1964), a woman who experienced the trauma of colonization in Australia: "Let no one say the past is dead. The past is all about us and within."[14] When a government apologizes to the survivors of the residential schools, as Canada's Federal Government did in June 2008, it is a positive first step acknowledging responsibility. When it immediately turns around and cuts funding to Aboriginal healing programs, there is a blatant, confusing mixed message sent.

Positive Steps

This story is nevertheless not entirely one of bleakness. There has been much wonderful positive action over the past decade. Many people and organizations are making a difference. The systemic healing of the transgenerational trauma of many generations is just beginning and that must not be forgotten. When there is several hundred years of systemic damage done, it may take just as long to heal the wounds. I do hope it moves along a little quicker than that. It is up to you and me, each of us, to create a critical mass that can influence government decision making. We benefit from the resourcefulness, talent and success of our ancestors and we have traditionally been eager to take on all those positive attributes. Now it is time to tap into the many great resources available to us to address the

---

13 The Honourable Justice Murray Sinclair. (2014). If you thought the truth was hard, reconciliation will be harder. Knight Lecture October 30th: University of Manitoba News. Retrieved from http://news.umanitoba.ca/if-you-thought-the-truth-was-hard-reconciliation-will-be-harder/
14 Oodgeroo Noonuccal (Kath Walker), (1964). We are going. Brisbane, AU: Jacaranda Press. In My People: A Kath Walker Collection. (1970). Brisbane, AU: Jacaranda Press, rev. eds. 1981, 1990, p 86.

emotional burdens passed down transgenerationally and left unresolved.[15] This invitation and journey is open to people all over the world today regardless of your context.

Family

---

15 Resources about the residential schools and healing actions, including resources for teachers and students, are found at www.trc.ca (The Truth and Reconciliation Commission of Canada), www.ahf.ca (The Aboriginal Healing Foundation) and www.aadnc-aandc.gc.ca (Indigenous and Northern Affairs Canada). The latter has an excellent timeline of relevant dates and events since the time The Royal Commission on Aboriginal Peoples filed its 1996 report and brought the experiences of former residential school students to national attention. Library and Archives Canada's Truth and Reconciliation Commission Web Archive is located at http://www.bac-lac.gc.ca/eng/discover/aboriginal-heritage/Pages/truth-reconciliation-commission-web-archive.aspx

SEPTEMBER

Systemic Healing

Written September 8, 2014

Systemic healing for human beings frequently runs counter to much in the scientific quantitative study of health. However, it doesn't need to, it just seems to be the reality. Scientific study does not like uniqueness, preferring similarity for the purposes of generalization. It tends to look at one aspect of the human being at a time. It studies one narrow theme expecting to find answers that are relevant for a whole system that is immensely complex and interconnected. Systemic healing looks at the whole, rather than the component parts. It embraces the physical, mental, emotional, spiritual, financial and relational dynamics of human beings. It focuses on the greater family system within a transgenerational context. Each situation is different. Systemic healing looks at all the systems that surround and influence the life of the person and their family system. One of the limitations of scientific study is that it continually seeks commonalities or similarities to back hypotheses. When a particular event "Z" occurs, "X" number of times, out of "Y" possibilities, we can say there is some degree of correlation. Scientific study often leaves out the idiosyncrasies of human experience. It often drops the outliers, which can be so illuminating. It makes an effort to leave out the impact of the researcher(s). It endeavours to leave out the spiritual dynamics of being human. It attempts to leave out emotion, which is fundamental to all human experience.

Quantitative empirical studies have an important role to play in the gathering of knowledge. We have all benefited from this type of research and inquiry. However, there is a tendency to avoid uniqueness unless you are the one in a million with some rare condition. Uniqueness is frowned upon because it doesn't lead to correlation. Empirical study records what can be seen or observed. The unseen, or that which cannot be observed, is deemed irrelevant in many studies regardless of how important it might be to the understanding of the overall picture. There is still a great deal of mystery around the human condition. We are unique spiritual beings living a human lifetime filled with emotional experiences. We understand the world around us through emotions. Every event, situation or relationship is interpreted through emotions – a wide range of emotions. Our bodies interact with stimuli from the external world, through feelings and sensations, and we use emotion to give it meaning. Of all the millions of pieces of information we are exposed to in every moment, we use filters developed through past emotional experiences and events to decide what is important to us and what is not. Many of these decisions are unconscious. We filter out stimuli that is deemed unimportant to us and let it go. We may let it go, however, it still exists. Others may find these pieces of information that we reject as highly valuable in their world and they store them in their body.

Much of the stimuli that comes our way to be processed is not even acknowledged or recognized because of the limitations of conscious human capacity. Much stimuli exists and is stored even if we are unable to process it with our visual, auditory or sensory systems. For instance, the vast spectrums of sound, colour and light that exist are well beyond our interpretative capacities at this time. We can experience and interpret only a narrow range of these spectrums. Like sound, colour and light, there is much mystery in our world that influences us in ways we don't yet understand. There is much in the universe that we are unable to process at this point in human development. Someday that may change. That does not mean we should ignore the mystery or pretend it doesn't exist. We are still impacted by what we cannot integrate at this time and we need to be open to new possibilities in everything we do.

As mentioned above, the scientific study of wellbeing is often very different than the concept of systemic healing. We take in information from our environment and store our experiences and interpretations of life as emotions in the body. While these processes are energetic and chemical in nature, the scientific world frequently sacrifices the emotional dynamic to achieve empirical data. If emotion is considered, it is often fragmented into a dozen or so commonly grouped emotions and the vital uniqueness and context of an experience is stripped away. Many studies eliminate what makes us uniquely human.

Human Uniqueness

Each human body is unique. Even identical twins are unique through the epigenetic expression of their genes and experience. While identical twins have vast similarity, they also develop wide diversity. Epigenetics reveals a unique transgenerational emotional inheritance. There might be similarities that can be generalized about human beings within a similar context, however, systemic healing taps into the concept that the wellness of the human body is contextual. Each human being carries the transgenerational trauma of their family system in a different way. I believe that each human body uniquely carries the messages to heal itself and regenerate, and also to encourage it to move forward in life toward greater spiritual development and growth.

As a spiritual being living a human experience, it is most important that you take responsibility for your own wellbeing. The journey meant for you is different than every other human journey. To attain wellbeing, you are encouraged to listen to the language of your body and to interpret its messages. Your body is customized to provide you with all that you wanted to experience in this lifetime. It is there as a vehicle for your spiritual development and growth. Body conditions and symptoms, and life challenges, are there for expansion. They are an opportunity to express communion between the body, mind, heart and spirit. Body conditions and symptoms are certainly not about punishment, as many believe. As the greater system seeks to balance itself, symptoms, conditions and behaviours sometimes bring attention to past family victims and perpetrators. They may highlight family members who are missing or excluded.

Symptoms and conditions can reflect atonement related to the behaviour or emotional experiences of another family member; perhaps one, two or three generations back, to balance the family system. Atonement is not punishment, it is an energetic action to balance the greater family system. I encourage you to build a relationship with any symptoms or conditions you may have, and to listen to the messages they provide. They may assist you in achieving systemic healing. To understand systemic healing, it is important to gain insight about the unresolved emotional trauma carried in the body of each family member from generation to generation. What transgenerational trauma has been passed from generation to generation? What messages for emotional resolution have been passed down as well? Some messages of the body may be sent by the greater family system to heal and release guilt, anger, hatred, sadness, shame, grief or atonement that has lingered unresolved for generations. Shifting your perspective from a narrow, compartmentalized view of your body and the conditions you experience, toward a broad expansive worldview, is essential. As a human being you are unique and the systemic healing appropriate for your situation is unique. Be very aware that you live within a greater family system that continually seeks to balance itself and it also impacts your systemic healing and wellbeing.

Part of the Whole

The greater family system ensures that all members of the family system are welcomed and included in the system. Everyone has a right to belong regardless of what they may have done or not done. There is no tolerance of exclusion. We all have a place in our family system and a specific role to play in this lifetime. Energetic ties or entanglements link family members to one another. Family members are not only connected through blood and DNA. They may be connected through energetic situations and events. For example, the victim is connected to the perpetrator, and their family systems become entangled with one another. Family members are also connected through epigenetic emotional inheritance that passes down the family system from generation to generation. Sometimes these entanglements serve us well and in other situations they keep us from moving forward in a healthy way. Healing actions of family members serve the development and growth of the greater family system. As one member of your family system, you can take the initiative to set transformation in motion. Sometimes you can observe the change that is occurring and sometimes you plant the seed without any sense of the difference you have initiated or made. Sometimes you are a catalyst and the consequences occur at a time well off into the future. It is important for your own wellbeing to let go of any attachment to the outcome. Your family system is unique from other family systems in that it seeks to fulfill the development and growth of that specific group of human beings and their souls. These family systems are interconnected through a greater universal electromagnetic field of energy that flows through each of our bodies; connecting each one of us to other human beings and their family systems, connecting us to the creatures of the wild around us and our environment; and simultaneously spiraling outward through space.

Purpose of Symptoms

The symptoms, conditions and life challenges you experience are there to provide you with an opportunity for growth. It is up to you to decide how to respond to them. You can explore, expand and be creative; or you can live through fear in a rigid, highly controlled world. Your symptoms are a message from your unconscious mind, since you wouldn't consciously create symptoms for yourself, and they manifest to move you forward in life. They provide you with information to help you fulfill your life goals for development and growth. They may bring new people into your life or help you shift direction if you have wandered a little too far from the goals you wanted to experience in this lifetime.

You are served best when you befriend the symptoms of your body. Take the time to understand why the symptom has appeared and what is sustaining or holding the symptom in place energetically. Sort out whether the symptom or condition is mimicking or reflecting something from your family system. In systemic constellations, representatives for symptoms are generally experienced as benevolent, and they frequently serve the individual or the greater family system in some way. Symptoms may be telling you that you have unhealthy relationships that need to shift into healthy relationships. Symptoms and conditions may be a way to shift your life direction and path. Symptoms may be prodding you to change your behaviour when it isn't serving your highest good. For example, if you continually get colds and flu, it's likely a message to slow yourself down and take care of yourself. Take some time to smell the roses!! The message is clear that you are doing too much, you are stressing your immune system and adrenals, and you need to change your lifestyle in some way. You need to listen more intently to your deep inner voice. This is particularly important in the rush of the world today. If you ignore these messages, the body may bring more aggressive or threatening symptoms forward to get your attention. That is the risk you take when you ignore your deep inner voice. If you will, the symptoms get louder or more in your face to get your attention. They become harder to ignore. This mindset is opposite to the mindset of modern medicine. Medicine says you are sick and need to be cured or fixed. Your immune system is compromised because you have a virus or bacteria present. To the detriment of many, diagnosis tends to shut down energetic and emotional exploration.

Within systemic healing, symptoms may be present to help you belong to your family system. They may be present to raise awareness that someone or something is missing in your family system. Look to your family system for answers. Did the onset of your symptoms correspond to some emotional time or event in your life? Do they correspond to a big anniversary in your family system, perhaps a birth, death or tragedy? When you take responsibility for your own wellbeing you also begin to care about the overall wellbeing of your family system and all those in it. Has someone been excluded or forgotten in your family system? This might be a few generations back. You might need to do a meaningful ritual to welcome any excluded family members back into the family system. Think of the many ways that you can improve your own relationships within your family system. Has something been silenced or is something being avoided? Bring the issue into the light. Take time to address the issue. Set up a ritual to shift the energy around the concern. Symptoms may recede if you listen to the messages, relate them to your own life and your family system and act to change something. If you have ignored the messages of the symptoms and conditions for too long, there may be consequences. If you want to read further on the subject of symptoms and conditions, Book 1 of this series, *Connect With Your Ancestors*, has a chapter on Chronic Illness and Emotional Stress or Trauma.

Embrace Systemic Healing

Systemic healing calls for an expanded mindset. It suggests that your immune system is susceptible to a virus or bacteria because you have unresolved emotional issues to address. You may have an internal battle going on that compromises your immune system. You may be rejecting your mother or your father and consequently rejecting Self. You may be engaging in self-abandonment. You may be living in agency with others, putting their needs before your own. Some emotional energetic entanglement from the past may be causing you to stress yourself out or push yourself too hard. Unconscious motivators or fears may be driving your life in some way. Pay attention to the heavy transgenerational trauma emotions you carry within you such as anger, rage, sorrow, grief, resentment, guilt or shame. They may be driving you in directions that don't serve your highest good. You may have unresolved childhood bonding issues or ancestral emotional trauma that needs attention. If you leave your body empty emotionally, perhaps engaging in addictive behaviours, malignant entities may make themselves at home within that empty space. You may find that the cells of your body have been stewing in a malignant soup filled with unhealthy ingredients for far too long. These unhealthy ingredients are heavy emotional energies, often referred to as negative energies. Any soup made with unhealthy ingredients will tend to make you sick. If you continue to feed the cells of your body unhealthy soup over the long-term, your body may become even more unwell. Take action. Throw out that malignant soup and begin a fresh pot with healthy ingredients. Create a healthy emotional soup for the cells of your body so that you may thrive and live life fully.

Unconscious Mind

The unconscious mind speaks to you with messages through symptoms, conditions and behaviours when it is time to address a specific issue within your life or family system. Something will trigger a remembering. The unconscious mind - the body - may attempt to reach you over and over if you ignore the first subtle messages. Be aware that you can neither ignore the messages without peril nor leave your family system behind. You might physically attempt to leave your family system behind by moving a long distance away or by stopping all communication with your family members, however, you can't energetically leave your family system behind. You cannot energetically separate. You are connected for this lifetime, energetically entangled, and the unwellness of one family member impacts the level of wellness of others. Your wellbeing is found through your greater family system, with those you chose as your parents and with all the others, like your siblings, if you have any, with whom you chose to share this lifetime. In an act of self-preservation, the unconscious mind may be informing you through symptoms, conditions and behaviours that action is needed for your highest good and for the common good and balance of the greater family system. The symptom is a message from your unconscious mind, which is imprinted or stored in the cells of your body. The messages become stronger over time if you ignore them. Symptoms may return over and over, become more intense, group together with additional symptoms, set rigidly in place to await your response, spread to other parts of the body or set up as repetitive behaviours. This is your unconscious mind's way of communicating with you that something needs to change or shift in your way of being. What needs to shift may be conscious or unconscious to you. It you are like many others, you may be engaging with your symptoms reactively rather than proactively or preventatively. If there is a symptom, condition or repetitive behaviour issue, it is definitely time to explore rather than ignore. Investigate your greater family system for the emotional origins of the symptom, condition or behaviour. Is the symptom reflecting something in your family system? Be aware that medical or psychological diagnosis may shut down this vital exploration. When you receive a diagnosis, you often stop wondering and exploring, and assume the answer to your problem has been found. To understand your symptoms, you are encouraged to tap into your imagination, your unconscious mind, your deep inner Self and your connection with your greater family system and ancestors. Does your symptom provide you with symbolic or metaphoric meaning that requires a little extra reflection or introspection? Perhaps you need to consult with others to gain a broad perspective. When did the symptom start? What happened in your life emotionally in the year prior to the onset? What is the symptom connected to emotionally? To develop the expanded worldview of systemic healing you need to step outside the box to explore the mystery beyond its boundaries.

Emotional Inheritance

When the message of the symptom is elusive, tap into the phenomenological approach of systemic constellations or engage in energetic and body focused practices to help with insight or to provide a new image. You are asked to look at any unresolved emotional trauma of your parents and ancestors that may have been transmitted down to you transgenerationally. What they left unprocessed and unresolved emotionally may be carried in your body. If you find yourself with repetitive life patterns that don't serve you well, that keep you from succeeding in life or stop you from moving forward in life, that seem to have a life of their own, or that block the flow of love in your life or family system, then it's time to check the health of your relationships with your parents and ancestors. Unhealthy relationships often stem from unhealthy energy boundaries with others. This includes unhealthy boundaries with the living and the dead. For more on boundary setting, please see the following few chapters. Unhealthy relationships often reveal emotional and non-life giving energetic entanglements with both the living and the dead. Who or what is calling to be seen? Who or what is calling to be heard? What relationships need to be shifted? What actions do you need to take for systemic healing to occur for you and your greater family system? As you read this book, I encourage you to journal your thoughts and moments of great insight for further reflection.

Family

Healthy Boundary

Written September 16, 2014

Do you have a healthy porous energy boundary? Do you maintain a healthy boundary in your relationships? There may be unresolved emotional trauma lingering from the past creating unhealthy boundaries, entanglements and challenging relationships with those who are living, and also with those who have died in the physical world and transitioned to the other side. The residue of this old emotional trauma sits in the body of a descendant, impacting the relationships they have with everyone around them. When relationships aren't healthy, you may receive messages from your unconscious mind through relationship difficulties, you may experience physical or mental health issues, you may be challenged with continuous money or financial difficulties, you may wander through life feeling spiritually lost, or you may feel emotionally paralysed, or alternatively, like an emotional mess. You may feel that you don't belong or fit anywhere. You may feel like a square peg attempting to fit into a round hole. Oh, you laugh, "I don't bother with those pesky emotions." Please read on.

What Messages?

While engaged in your human experience, it is often difficult to link or piece together your life purpose on this planet. Confounded, many people remain at a very superficial level of existence. It is valuable to understand that you are being guided along your journey. You are not left to flounder by the greater collective field around you. Still, you need to understand that you do have to make decisions and take actions to move forward. No one is going to do that for you. Sometimes unfortunate or sudden surprises occur in your life when you refuse to make decisions, or you sit on the fence refusing to move forward for too long. These may happen over and over too. The greater collective field is just attempting to jump start your mind, body, heart and spirit. Remember that there are no wrong decisions. Although, you may find yourself on lengthy detours with some of the decisions you make and actions you take. You receive messages from the greater collective unconscious and you are continually receiving messages from your unconscious mind. These messages are sent to you as symptoms, conditions and relationship issues from the body. If you are stuck in your rational conscious mind, believing that it is everything, you are missing a relationship with your far more powerful unconscious mind - your body. The messages of the unconscious mind may be symbolic or metaphoric. They may need some creative interpretation. These messages are highly contextual to your own human situation. It is a little like dream interpretation. There is some general information in books to provide some guidance, however, it may not be accurate for your situation. Sometimes you may need a little outside guidance to help you piece the messages together. That's the work I do with my clients. I am able to separate the messages put forward by your unconscious mind from the chatter of your rational conscious mind. Your body, heart and soul get very excited when your conscious mind pays attention to these messages. This is something you can learn to do for yourself. It's part of learning self-love and what I call systemic healing. It is a skill that the baby has when it arrives on the planet until the adults around him or her shut down this valuable talent with rational chatter. I hope the day will come when parents and teachers will have the capacity to teach children to interpret the language and messages of their unconscious mind - their own body - or just to allow it to happen naturally. First, it will require each adult to do their own emotional and spiritual healing work so that the journey of systemic healing will be understood. You cannot teach what you do not know.

Although I routinely refer to symptoms, I prefer to call the communication from the unconscious mind "benevolent messages" rather than "symptoms". People continually speak of fighting their symptoms, doing battle with their symptoms or conquering their symptoms. That is language that extends from the "Might Makes Right"[16] era of human development. It is arrogant language. That language no longer serves us well. The world has

---

16 Rauhut, N. (n.d.). Thrasymachus (fl. 427 B.C.E.). *Internet Encyclopedia of Philosophy*. Retrieved February 20, 2018 from http://www.iep.utm.edu/thrasymachus/

shifted and "might" is no longer considered "right" in the world, although many people have yet to acknowledge this or realize it. It's time for each of us to open to an enormous energetic shift, and to take a humbler stance, bowing to the infinite wisdom and language of our body/mind.

I encourage others to befriend these messages from the unconscious mind, not fight them. Internal conflict often leads to unwellness and weakening of the immune system. You may feel that this is easier said than done. You may be caught up in a societal norm "doing battle with your symptoms," or you may be in denial of the severity of your symptoms. Many others let their symptoms possess them and create an identity for them. They refer to their conditions in the possessive form, it is "my cancer" or "my arthritis." They cannot envision themselves or life without these symptoms. The symptoms are entangled with their identity. "All the women in my family battle breast cancer." Surrendering to their symptoms, and listening to the messages they deliver, is the farthest thing from their mind. Although I realize it can be difficult, this mindset needs to transform. If you are caught up in the rigid limitations of the terminology and vocabulary used in the medical world or psychological realm, it is time to broaden your worldview using a systemic approach, or at least integrating a systemic approach. I suggest that referring to messages rather than symptoms is a healthier way to engage with the language of your body. Feel free to call these messages of the body whatever you choose.

This discussion started out with the development of healthy boundaries. It requires a person to listen to the messages of their body and use discernment to create a healthy porous boundary with others. When boundaries are unhealthy, you may let others walk all over you, or you may build up a solid wall of emotional armour. You may walk all over the boundaries of others. If you are not listening to the messages of your body, you may not have a strong sense of your own boundaries with Self or with others. When there are unhealthy boundaries, the cells of your body stew in a malignant soup of ingredients – anger, rage, regret, pain, sadness, resentment, shame, guilt, anxiety, depression, unhappiness, sorrow or grief – the list is long. Without healthy porous boundaries, relationships tend to feel problematic with a great amount of drama to address. You are encouraged to explore any heavy emotions that are stored in the cells of your body. Sometimes these heavy emotions linger for decades, with your cells continually stewing in this unhealthy soup. You begin to receive messages from your body such as cancer, adrenal fatigue, chronic fatigue, heart conditions or other immune conditions. When these heavy emotions linger beyond their usefulness, often from very early childhood experiences – perhaps preconception, prenatal, perinatal or postnatal - and they keep relationships from being life giving, then it is time to evaluate the energy boundary you maintain for yourself. It is time to replace these heavy emotions with a journey to the lighter side of the emotional spectrum. It is time to experience joy, happiness, awe, contentment, hope, curiosity, enthusiasm, gratitude, kindness, love, cheerfulness, peacefulness, confidence, satisfaction, grace, enjoyment and abundance. It is your choice! Sometimes your choice is being limited or blocked by the transgenerational trauma you carry for others in your family system. If that is the case, then it is time to first work through all this transgenerational trauma, so you are free to step into the light.

What Boundary You Ask?

When you learn to develop a strong healthy boundary, you learn to care for yourself first. This means you stay out of agency with others. You learn to put your needs before the needs of others in everything you do. You stop living through duty and obligation and begin living through love. When your needs are met then you can assist others from a place of wellbeing. This isn't selfish behaviour - it's healthy self-love. It is energy sustaining rather than energy deadening behaviour. Your body won't have to deliver as many benevolent messages to encourage you to change your attitudes, your behaviours, your direction or your way of being in the world.

Energetic Entanglements

Energetic entanglements that are not serving you well mess with your ability to maintain a healthy boundary. If you need some help understanding your own boundaries, you may attain insight about any unhealthy entanglements through systemic and family constellations or by drawing a genosociogram of your family system. A genosociogram is a family tree with all the big events of your family ancestry – all the trauma, the tragedy, the oppression, the synchronicities, the deaths that occurred too young and the emotional response patterns that are evident. When the energy boundaries are not healthy between generations, the unresolved emotional trauma passes from generation to generation. Developing a healthy boundary means severing any unhealthy energetic entanglements. It means shifting unhealthy relationships with the living or dead into healthy relationships. You may consciously or unconsciously maintain these entanglements out of love and loyalty to your family system. The children in family systems sacrifice themselves all the time in this way. They unconsciously sacrifice their own wellbeing to take care of their mother or father emotionally. Children are willing to sacrifice their own wellbeing for a lifetime, taking on symptoms and conditions for the whole family system. The child can be the family scapegoat, with the energy of other family members being, "better you than me." Creating a healthy boundary means acknowledging when you are transgenerationally carrying a burden for, or sharing a burden with, your parents, ancestors or other family members. Remember these family members or relationships may or may not be related to you through blood. They may be energetic family members. They may not just be individuals but whole groups of people as well. For example, if your ancestors were involved in harming large groups of people in the past, you may be aligned energetically with those that suffered, carrying the energy of the victim. Those who suffered in the past at the hands of a family member become part of your family system and these situations need to be acknowledged and emotionally addressed. You may be aligned with the family members that harmed others. We can be aligned energetically with the victims or the perpetrators. These entanglements may be with individuals, events, institutions, societies or situations that created conscious or unconscious unresolved emotional family or ancestral trauma or wounds, within the family and/or community. Some examples of these energetic family entanglements include:

- Aborted, miscarried or stillborn children;

- Anyone who died young or tragically;

- Perpetrators of harm done to you (now or ancestrally);

- People you have harmed or bullied, or people who have harmed or bullied you, in the home, schools, workplaces or religious institutions, etc. (now or ancestrally);

- Former significant partners in your life, or the lives of your parents, grandparents or great grandparents;

- Significant unrequited love interests;

- Excluded, shunned, forgotten or missing family members;

- Those institutionalized in orphanages, residential schools, prisons or mental health centres;

- Unacknowledged children;

- Anyone not mourned in an appropriate way and there is a lingering feeling of incompletion;

- Those who commit suicide;

- Religious institutions that create fear or exclusion;

- Those comrades who died in war;

- Those killed in war;

- Those you or your ancestors killed in war;

- Situations of regret;

- Situations of survivor guilt;

- The "enemy" in any situation;

- Those who gained or lost fortunes;

- Those with addictive behaviours;

- Injustices around inheritances;

- The guilt of the bystander;

- Those injured by bombs that dropped;

- Those who dropped the bombs;

- Countries of origin and new homelands;

- Immigrants who suffered in their ancestral homeland;

- Energetically harmful government regulation; and,

- Relationships through oaths or initiations.

It is important to address the unresolved emotional entanglements of your family system, community and greater society. Lack of action or silence may increase the impact on future generations.

Connecting to Self

If you're not connected to your authentic inner Self, you may not be attuned to your boundary. You may spend most of your time in your head, or outside your body altogether. You may be split off energetically, dissociated or out wandering in the etheric field that surrounds your body. There may be a heavy layer of unresolved emotional trauma covering over or hiding your authentic Self. To shift the entanglements related to unresolved emotional trauma or wounds, you are encouraged to get connected to your body. You are encouraged to ground yourself to Mother Earth by connecting with the natural world around you. You are encouraged to ground yourself with your ancestors, the foundation of your wellbeing. You are part of your precise family system for a reason and you chose to experience this human journey with this particular family system. There is a great amount of inner development and growth found through the contemplation of why you chose these unique individuals to share this lifetime.

Grounding requires you to develop a strong healthy porous personal energy boundary. You learn to care for yourself first before considering the needs of others. This means you stop self-abandoning. This involves developing compassion for Self or self-love, using self-soothing techniques, and you learn to self-parent. Anything you feel you did not get from your parents you seek as an adult from within Self. You let go of further expectations and you let go of blame and judgement. This involves getting connected with the energy and emotions held in your body, whether it feels comfortable, numb or uncomfortable inside. If you remain connected to your deep inner Self, or routinely re-connect with it, you understand when to say YES and when to say NO. If you struggle to make decisions in life, you may not be living firmly within your body listening to the messages it provides for you. It is important to feel your body's emotional response to any question asked of you or any decision you need to make. If you say YES, then begin to feel resentment or anger rising, then it's likely time to shift that response to NO. You listen to your body when it gets tight, contracted, feels tension or pressure, has aches or pains, is unable to take in air, feels tied in knots, gives you a headache, feels nauseated or sick, feels stuck in life, has chronic symptoms and so forth. Ringing in your ears is the body's way of asking you to pick up the communication line – it's time to connect. The body wants you to listen to the messages it is delivering. If you hear ringing, ask your body to slow down the message so you can receive it over the next day or two, and then be open and prepared to listen. These messages from the body are asking you to shift something in your life. Listen and take action, and your body will love you for it. It is the beginning of a trusting relationship. It is the beginning of self-love. The first step is building a healthy relationship with Self, and that requires a healthy energy boundary. If you haven't done so already, I encourage you to develop one and to feel it within your body. The chapter in this book called *Love Yourself Through Boundary Setting* illustrates ways to develop a healthy energy boundary. Boundary setting is a skill that can be learned through practise.

Envision Your Boundary

Set a healthy boundary around yourself, feeling it like a tropical island of love, and then decide who you want to invite onto your island. Also, decide who gets to come to the shoreline of your island for further investigation or who you want to have anchor further offshore until an invitation is extended. If you listen, you will know inside that there are others you definitely do not want to invite onto your island. Sometimes there are people who you sense intentionally drain your energy or perhaps mean to harm you in some way. Perhaps they have hurt you repeatedly in the past. You might want to keep those people away from your island altogether. Of course, this is tricky if the person is a close family member. You cannot energetically exclude family members without consequences so the development of healthy energy boundaries is mandatory. The shoreline of the island - perhaps it is a beach - is your healthy energetic boundary. You want it to be porous like a sandy beach or soft enough to allow those you love to come closer, yet firm enough to keep the ones who make you feel tense and unwell, further away. If you have built a twenty-foot fence around your island to keep everyone out, you likely have some boundary work to do to soften that rigid position. If you built a solid fortress on your island to protect yourself, you may have to soften your emotional armour to be in relationships with others. You are meant to be in relationships during your human experience. You are also meant to take some time to be alone on your island in the silence and to engage in introspection. If you let everyone party like crazy on your island whenever they want, you may want to do some boundary work to create a boundary where one presently doesn't exist. Listen to your inner voice. You may now be wondering, "Where did I get this rigid boundary?" or "Why don't I have a boundary?" To be more helpful, perhaps the question is more accurately, "Why don't I have a healthy porous boundary?"

Learning Boundary Setting

Our current energetic boundary habits were set in our early relationship with our biological mother, whether you were raised by her or not, and then it was likely reinforced by other caregivers. Did you get too much of mother energetically or not enough? Our deep inner fears and energetic boundary are intertwined with mother and her emotional wellbeing. There is no blame or judgment as we look back; rather we seek to develop compassion for all the emotional journeys of those who came before us. What was mother experiencing emotionally when you were conceived, when you were in the womb, at birth or in early childhood? Was she anxious or upset about being a mother? Was she worried about your wellbeing within the womb? Did she experience complications at any stage of pregnancy? What was going on for maternal grandmother when she was carrying your mother in the womb? Was life safe for her? Was she in a stable loving relationship or was she fearful about her future? Was she well supported by maternal grandfather and others? What were your mother and grandmother carrying emotionally and energetically in their bodies for their family systems? Whatever grandmother experienced was likely passed transgenerationally down to mother. Whatever mother experienced was likely passed transgenerationally down to you and your siblings. What fears do you have that seem irrational or without basis? What fears do you carry in life that developed in your early relationship with your mother? Remember that her fears became your fears. What unconscious inner fears do you carry in life that impact everything you do? Do you carry fear of failure, fear of being alone, fear of success, fear of being adventurous, or any other fear that keeps you from moving forward in life? How are these inner fears impacting your energy boundary with others? Are you asking for too much from others? Do you avoid others? This might be a good opportunity to do some journaling.

Perhaps you had an emotionally unavailable mother. She may have been there physically for you every day but absent emotionally. She was there for you physically every day making sure you were clothed and fed, however, she may not have felt supported by her partner or she may have carried unresolved emotional trauma of her own through her family system, keeping her feeling wounded and in a state of emotional distance. You may have unconsciously felt abandoned in early childhood because of this. You would have developed emotional response strategies to survive that feeling of abandonment. That's a common feeling for many people. This level of abandonment may be slight or quite pronounced. For some people, they feel this abandonment as a lack of safety. This reflection on early life is not about blaming or judging mother. In fact, it's about honouring and gaining compassion for mother and her journey. It's about acknowledging what you experienced and learning from it, then letting the rest go. It is time to let go of each story you creatively build up as a child around events that occurred in your life. It is time to shift from the narrow perspective of the child to the expansive perspective of an emotionally mature adult. You don't need to forget what happened; however, you do need to take a look at the big picture. It is time to create a healthy porous energy boundary around yourself and with your mother. Let the new, healthy, energetic distance between you and your mother be the love between you. As you look back, you take what you can learn from the past to shift your present and influence your future.

Too Little or Too Much

On the one hand, you may feel like you got too little energetically from mother, like you didn't get enough, and you likely continued to self-abandon throughout childhood and into adulthood. Are there ways that you betray yourself by ignoring your inner voice? What deep inner fears and perceptions do you live by? Who do they belong to in your family system? These inner fears are life limiting and the list can be long. I'm worthless. I'm not good enough. I'm alone. I don't deserve love. I'm not wanted. I'm no one. I'm afraid to show up. I'm invisible. I'm vulnerable. I'm a fraud. I'm stupid. I'm ugly. I'm a failure. I'm a victim. I don't deserve to take up space. I'm not lovable. I'm overwhelmed. I'm not worthy of love. The inner fears we live by are highly contextual within our own family system, and they frequently pass from generation to generation. Our boundary is defined and developed by the inner fears we carry in our body, unless we change those inner fears. In response to feelings of abandonment or aloneness, you may continually draw in others to have your emotional needs met. You may draw in others that are not in your highest interest. In response to numbness, you may feel nothing as others cross into your energy field. Of course, you may not feel worthy of having more. You may find that you feel ambivalent to this discussion about healthy energy boundaries. You may feel totally disconnected from your body and your energy boundary. This is common if you spend all your time in your head intellectualizing, rationalizing or worrying. Do not misunderstand me, we are all meant to have certain fears in life, they tend to keep us alive, nevertheless, it is time to minimize how the inner fears that seem irrational impact your life.

On the other hand, if you got too much of mother, such as in situations where mother never let go of you energetically, she may have kept you close to help ease her own inner feelings of pain or loneliness. Helicopter parents are a good example of this today. If you are not familiar with the term "helicopter parent," I pulled a definition from Oxford Dictionaries Online:

> "A parent who takes an overprotective or excessive interest in the life of their child or children: some college officials see all this as the behaviour of an overindulged generation, raised by helicopter parents and lacking in resilience. Origin 1980s: from the notion of the parent 'hovering' over the child or children."[17]

Helicopter parents don't tend to give their children the opportunity to experience failure. Helicopter parents give their children little independence and they are still heavily involved in the lives of their children even when they are adults. Helicopter parents may carry the inner fears of not feeling loved, feeling like failures or feeling alone, and they unconsciously provide the opposite emotional situation for their children to compensate

---

17 Helicopter parent. (2015). English Oxford Living Dictionaries Online. Retrieved September 15, 2017 from https://en.oxforddictionaries.com/definition/helicopter_parent

for their own wounds. It is a rejection of their own parents and their parenting styles. If this is or was your situation, you may have developed a feeling of being flooded emotionally by mother and/or father. If you are unconsciously carrying their emotional burdens for them, their sense of overwhelm or failure, perhaps feeling a lack of safety or carrying their yearnings for love, you may feel like you got too much from them energetically. Sometimes the child feels like their role in the family is to hold mother and father's relationship together. This may make the child feel like they got too much of mother and/or father energetically. If your place in the family was between mother and father, keeping the peace or mediating, you may feel energetically overwhelmed. This is far too much for any child to carry. You are energetically too close. You may still be trapped within the energy boundaries of mother and/or father without an energy boundary of your own. You may not have individuated well from mother and/or father as your life progressed. Your sense of Self may not have developed well. You may still feel the presence of your mother and/or father heavily in your life. To unconsciously create some energetic space for yourself, you may respond in relationships by pushing others away or you may avoid being in relationships altogether.

Practise, Practise!!

A strong healthy boundary is flexible enough to allow you to interact with others, porous enough when needed to let loved ones in closer without needing to push them away, and firm enough to keep others out without maintaining a fortress of armour around you, when the body says the answer is a firm NO. You need to have healthy boundaries with both the living and the dead. I guide clients through activities in boundary awareness and suggest boundary setting as a daily practice for them with everyone who enters their energy field. Just like a musician who needs to practise daily to master their instrument, each human being needs to practise boundary setting daily until they become masters at listening to the messages of their own body with adult maturity. You might be wondering why we aren't born with healthy boundaries? Learning boundary setting is a part of the spiritual development and growth you wanted to experience in this lifetime on planet Earth. In the spiritual realm, you experience unconditional love. You are guaranteed unconditional pure love. Your deep inner soul chose a human lifetime to experience feelings of separation, emotional trauma, fears, woundedness, exclusion and other human conditions. You gain a greater understanding of your energy boundaries and the value within the struggles you have experienced when you accept that you chose to experience these issues in this lifetime. You chose many of the individuals (souls) who have provided, or will eventually provide, these challenging experiences. With acceptance of this concept, you can find alternative ways of being in relationship with others through healthy energy boundaries. You can transform your world!

Symptoms Create a Boundary

Written September 27, 2014

Many physical, psychological, emotional, mental, spiritual, and relationship conditions, symptoms and challenges create an unconscious boundary for an individual. This is especially evident when the individual doesn't have a healthy strong porous energetic boundary in life. In its infinite wisdom, the unconscious mind, which is imprinted in the cells of the body, provides a symptom or condition that serves the individual's highest good, or it may serve to balance or heal the wounds of the greater family system. Symptoms or messages of the body are gifts in strange wrapping.

It's hard to envision many symptoms being benevolent, however, in the field of systemic healing that utilizes systemic constellations and body focused energy approaches, many symptoms support the client in one way or another. Systemic constellations are a visual and visceral way to set up any life issue. They are phenomenological in nature. It is like mapping out your life challenges in front of your eyes with live representatives or with markers. In a systemic constellation, you might set up the first representative as the Client and the second representative as the Symptom. Another way to set up the constellation is to set up the first representative as the Symptom and the second representative as the Message of the Symptom. The representatives are asked to go into their body and allow the slow movement of the field to occur. Each representative is asked what is going on for them, what they are experiencing, what they are feeling. Each representative is asked how they relate to the other representative. The representative for the Symptom may be a missing person in the family system, or it may morph into a parent or grandparent who remains close to the individual in some way, or it may be highlighting an unhealthy relationship that needs to shift. Symptoms may point to something unresolved in prior generations between the parents or grandparents. Unhealthy relationships or symptoms often reveal an energetic entanglement that needs to be addressed. In this way, the symptoms create a boundary, encouraging individuals to step out of these energetic entanglements. It is valuable to look at the origins of our energy boundaries and understand how symptoms create a boundary.

Boundary with Mother

Systemic healing asks you to be very honest with yourself and to let down the façade you have built up around yourself to serve your own emotional needs. It requires a shift from being closed to being open, from feeling in control to being vulnerable. This can be a painful process. It can hurt to look deeply at the reality of this most intimate of relationships. Our ability to go within may be restricted by the boundary we have developed around ourselves. There may be a wall of armour keeping us from going within to explore. Our energy boundaries initially develop in relationship to our mother. If mother had no boundary with others, you likely have no boundary with others. It's time to develop a strong healthy porous energy boundary. If she built a boundary of steel around herself so she wouldn't have to feel, you likely have a boundary of steel around your heart and inner Self. It's time to soften the edges of the boundary to allow loved ones to get closer to you if that is something you desire, or perhaps you are seeking greater intimacy with others. If mother unconsciously gained weight as a layer of emotional protection, you may also gain weight to unconsciously protect yourself emotionally. If mother didn't feel good about her body image, you may not either. It's time to develop a strong healthy porous energy boundary that is more life giving. Weight gain may have served to support you earlier in life in some way as emotional protection, however, once you learn self-love and maintain a healthy boundary it may no longer be needed. Please see the other chapters in this book on setting boundaries.

Looking further at the boundaries set through your early relationship with mother, if mother felt worthless, you may feel worthless, or fear being worthless, and likely compensate in your unconscious behaviours to keep from feeling worthless. You may work too much, take on too much responsibility, or live as a high achiever or perfectionist to prove you are enough. If mother felt alone and vulnerable, you may feel alone and vulnerable, or fear being alone and vulnerable, and compensate in your unconscious behaviours to keep from feeling alone or vulnerable. Relationships may trigger feelings of inadequacy or lack of safety. You may stay in relationships that are not life giving or you may be overly independent so that you don't have to rely on anyone. All of these ways of showing up in the world indicate that you lack a healthy energy boundary with Self and others.

Our lives are filled with unconscious behaviours and emotional strategies to help us overcome our deepest fears. Wellness comes when we sort out our deepest inner fears and stop living unconsciously and reactively through them. We can change these behaviours once we recognize that they originate somewhere else in our family system and understand what is holding them in place or contributing to them. When behaviours and symptoms create a boundary, it usually entails exploring our family system for unhealthy relationships, focusing on missing or excluded family members, listening to the messages of our body that show up as symptoms or conditions, investigating family emotional and behavioural patterns and sorting out the energetic entanglements in our life. Wellness comes when we take responsibility or take charge of our own wellbeing (notice I didn't say take control, which isn't possible) and stop letting fears rule our life. Many symptoms recede or diminish when an individual develops a strong healthy boundary with others, connects with their deep inner Self, connects with their parents and ancestors, releases burdens carried for others, releases fears and heavy emotions that have been dragged along throughout life, and engages in self-care, self-love, and self-parenting. This shift may vary depending on how long the symptom, condition or behaviour has manifested in your life. This transition is about embracing emotional and spiritual maturity. You can remain stubborn and stuck, clinging to the status quo, or you can move forward courageously into the unknown. If you are trapped in the narrow perspective of the child, remaining emotionally immature, you have the choice of shifting or stagnating. This generalization is made in recognition of all the beautiful loving children of the world who have transitioned to emotional maturity at a very early age, out of love and loyalty to their family system, noticeable by their early life struggles and challenges. For example, young children with cancer and tumours or immune system issues. Frequently, they sacrificed themselves to contribute to the balance and wellbeing of the greater family system. When the adults do their emotional healing work it tends to create an energetic shift for the child.

Symptoms Deliver Messages

When symptoms create a boundary, you are experiencing the gifts and talents of the unconscious mind. The unconscious ninety percent of the mind seems to be there as a support for human beings and frequently as a path to, or source of, wellbeing. The rational ten percent of the mind, with the ego along for the ride, loves the status quo and puts on the breaks at any sign of change or transition. You can choose to live solely through your small analytical rational mind or you can learn to explore the wonders of your expansive unconscious mind. You have a choice! The decision is up to you. An interesting observation is that the unconscious mind is reactive, so it needs to continually learn and store new ways of being. This can be achieved by experiencing new stimuli whenever possible to serve you well as you evolve as a human emotional and spiritual being.

The unconscious mind is there to help you improve your life and the wellbeing of the greater family system. It is filled with a wealth of valuable knowledge and you need to learn how to tap into this ancient pool of vital information. The unconscious mind may continue to provide messages as symptoms for you whether you ignore them or not. Listening to this inner voice, which has generally been immensely stifled the past few centuries, doesn't come easily to many human beings today. We tend to listen to external voices in our world or avoid listening altogether. We often seek entertainment as a distraction, so we don't have to listen to our deep inner voice. It is the inner voice that speaks to you with unconditional love. If you ignore it indefinitely, symptoms and conditions may begin to appear. The more you ignore that inner voice, the worse the symptoms grow to be.

When you ignore your deep inner voice indefinitely the symptoms multiple, metastasize, aggravate, intensify, increase, expand, return, worsen, and exacerbate – just to serve and support you, and to get your attention. Even worse, your symptoms may travel down the generations to your children and grandchildren. When you have symptoms, it's time to take responsibility and pay attention to these valuable body messages. Symptoms and challenges are a wake-up call. Many individuals finally begin to explore when they receive no satisfactory answers from the medical and psychological establishments. They may be told there is no cause or there is no cure. Others wait for a late stage diagnosis. Humans, with their egos firmly in place, love to resist change! They want someone else to find the answers. They want someone else to do the work for them. They want someone else to blame. Consequently, many people take their issues to their grave. When the cause of the symptom is unknown, and there is no quick cure or fix, many people begin to explore other options. That's when it's time to step courageously outside the programmed box you have been living within since childhood.

Symptoms as Boundaries

If you have symptoms that show up on your skin such as rashes or other skin conditions, or symptoms that impact your appearance, your body may be setting up a boundary for you. The message for you may be to develop a strong healthy boundary and it may raise the need to deal with issues of unworthiness, low self-esteem, feeling not good enough, inadequacy, the need for external validation, non-acceptance of Self, or feelings of invisibility. These symptoms want you to shift your way of showing up in the world. Your skin is your physical boundary with your environment and the world. Your skin continually picks up messages from the external environment. What needs to shift? It might be time to accept your full birthright and breathe in your full life force energy from your mother. That requires you to say YES to life as it was given to you and to accept your mother just the way she is or was. That's the healthy life-giving step that may have been missing at birth. It's time for you to give yourself permission to take up space and to take care of yourself first.

These inner feelings tend to rise out of unresolved relationship issues with your biological mother. Sometimes the attachment wound can be very subtle, such as a week away from mother in early life, or it can be more traumatizing. These issues seem to be common for individuals who are given up for adoption or fostering, or when they are not raised by mother due to other circumstances. In many situations, you may become the overachiever to prove your worthiness over and over. You rationalize in your conscious mind that these feelings in your body do not matter, that the relationship with biological mother does not matter. Your body can only take these behaviours for so long until the message is clear that you have to make changes in your life. Whether mother was there physically, but absent emotionally, or mother was absent physically in some way, you still have to sort through your unconscious emotional responses to that absence in your life, whether it is in your face or it doesn't seem like a big deal. You need to make room in your heart for your biological mother since she is fifty percent of whom you are inside. That is one of the greatest challenges for many in systemic healing. Without making room in your heart for your biological mother, you are rejecting fifty percent of yourself and you are also rejecting the long line of maternal lineage standing behind mother and there to support you. Emotional rejection of mother and Self invites immune issues – the body rejecting aspects of itself.

Symptoms That Remind

If you are an adult and you are still expecting one or both of your parents to change, or you are angry at a parent and expecting an apology, your body may provide you with symptoms, conditions or repetitive relationship issues to address. If you have to feel like you are controlling everything in life to feel safe, or to find certainty and structure, you may have symptoms that tighten or contract your body in stubbornness or rigidity. Relationship issues often create boundaries for you if you don't have a strong healthy boundary. You may reject a parent and attempt to do everything the opposite to them, or you may unconsciously merge with characteristics of the parent. It's time to develop a strong healthy boundary and relationship with that parent whether it takes place in the material world or not. A healthy relationship with healthy boundaries comes about through awareness of your relationship style, including feelings of getting too much from mother or not enough. A healthy relationship evolves through the development of compassion for the emotional journeys of our parents and grandparents, needing to accept them just the way they are or were.

Symptoms of Agency

If you have symptoms such as breast cancer; back issues; neck issues; or hand, wrist, elbow, arm or shoulder issues; your body may be telling you to start taking care of your own needs first before you do things for others. You may also be carrying transgenerational trauma for your family system, which is energy deadening. You may be living in agency. Do you nurture everyone but yourself? Do you take care of the needs of everyone else and ignore your own needs? You may have come into the world feeling like it was your role to take care of your mother's emotional needs and the pattern repeats itself in each new relationship. It may also pass from generation to generation. It's time to develop a strong, healthy, porous boundary that serves you well.

Symptoms of Inner Conflict

If you have immune system issues, you may have an internal conflict going on inside. Your body may be helping you to understand that you are rejecting mother or her family line, father or his family line, or both. Since your body is fifty percent mother and fifty percent father, a rejection of either or both is a rejection of Self. Are you lacking compassion for those who came before you? Do you struggle to take mother or father into your heart regardless of what they may or may not have done? What you reject about your mother or father, remembering that you chose these parents, you reject within your own body. Your body, through the use of your immune system, delivers messages by beginning to reject itself - creating immune issues. It reflects your own rejection of Self, through your rejection of mother. These symptoms create a boundary. They are messages from the unconscious that an unhealthy relationship or an energetic entanglement is being held or maintained by a rigid, inflexible inner image that usually developed in childhood. Some of these inner images can be residue of past lifetimes. You may find the same relationship images repeating in the current lifetime. In many situations, you don't have to explore a past life. When you listen to the unconscious language of your body you may find resolution within a couple current lifetime ancestral generations. Many symptoms are maintained in the cells of the body by heavy energies such as fears, rage, worry, resentment, anger, pain, sorrow, grief, guilt or shame. Many of these heavy energies settled into the body in relationship with parents or grandparents, and the emotional response patterns you have to them may be aimed at parents or grandparents, even if it is unconscious. We don't become unwell in isolation. We become unwell in relationship. You don't usually have to look far to find the source of your unwellness. When you listen, the answers tend to be within you. Seek assistance if you have a difficult time separating the unconscious language from the conscious rational language (the story you tell yourself over and over). You may have difficulty identifying family patterns because they have been lived for decades, and they have become normalized in your life.

Listen and Change

If you have symptoms that make you feel stuck in life; or that make you feel tight, stiff, or contracted in your body; or that keep you from feeling the energy flowing in your body; then it may be time to open to the wonders of the unknown world around you. You may be restricting yourself to living in a small world. It may be time to give an inch (or centimetre). If you have conditions or symptoms that make you want to stay home, make you miss opportunities that arise, make you want to go to bed to rest or lie down, or keep you from socializing, then the symptoms may be creating a boundary for you where one is presently absent. These symptoms may also be telling you to relax, to get connected with your inner Self or to create healthy boundaries around Self. The important part to know is that unhealthy boundaries can be shifted, and new healthy boundaries can be created and consistently maintained to achieve your highest goals and wellness. Boundary setting is internal not external. If you have a healthy boundary with parents, siblings, children, extended family members, friends, clients, patients, or co-workers, you individuate well from them. That means you can be in relationship with others and still maintain a strong sense of inner Self. You won't get lost in relationships. You will know if you have healthy boundaries if there is very little unnecessary drama in your relationships. You don't get caught up in the drama of others. You can step back emotionally from the drama of others. You don't require others to provide external feedback to help you feel good about yourself at a deep level within, or to know if you are emotionally well. The opinion of others is not relevant to your wellbeing. This is especially important for all the healers, helpers, servers, peacebuilders and frontline workers of the world. Many of you are seeking to heal yourself through your work with others. This is particularly important for those working in medical or psychological fields – the archetypal wounded healers of the world. Doesn't it feel great when you help fix the life of someone else! If you agreed with me, I am talking to you. No one needs to be fixed. No one is broken. Each person has a different journey with different challenges. Some people live heavy fates that feel very uncomfortable to others. Be aware that they are living the life they are meant to live. Each of us is responsible for changing our own lives. We cannot fix the life of another. Change comes from within. If you are attempting to fix the lives of others, be very aware that it is time to do your own emotional healing work, for this lifetime and transgenerationally, to keep from burning out or developing your own symptoms. Remember that healthy boundaries can definitely be established with those who are living or with those who have died or transitioned to the other side.

Yes or No

Healthy boundaries allow you to say YES or NO when you mean YES or NO. Healthy boundaries develop when you listen to the message of your body saying YES or NO, as you feel pulled by external requests for your time, energy and resources. You are able to listen to your deep inner voice, know what is right for yourself, and act on it. You know it is right because you feel peaceful, calm, joy filled or excited in a healthy way within your body. There is no inner tension in your body created by the decision you are making. There are no unwelcome anxious knots in your stomach. When you have a strong sense of Self, and you feel triggered emotionally by a person or an event, you will have a deep sense of how to self-soothe yourself to reduce the emotional charge. You can only change yourself, not others. What do you need to do in the moment for your own wellbeing? Self-love and self-care are the basis of healthy boundaries. You will know if you have a healthy boundary because it feels good to stay in your body - to stay present - without the desire to escape through addictive behaviours or to escape by splitting off or numbing emotionally or spiritually.

Stuck in Your Head

If you feel the desire to split off, fragment, dissociate, defend, rationalize or intellectualize, you likely don't have a healthy porous boundary or a strong sense of Self in the moment. Defensiveness may be used to take the place of a healthy self-boundary and getting stuck in your head intellectualizing is a type of defense. Intellectualizing is an escape from feeling. You don't have to be in your body feeling your emotions if you are intellectualizing. So, developing a strong sense of your boundary involves getting out of your head. Let the constant chatter in your head go and feel your emotional response with your body. Are you able to feel the energy flowing throughout your body, or are there energetic blocks keeping you numb or tense in some regions of your body? These regions of your body are emotional holding patterns usually developed very early in life. Having the capacity to remain comfortable with the feelings and emotions in your body as they arise, even if they are uncomfortable, and having a strong sense of Self, is essential to wellbeing and healing. Having a strong boundary in relationship with others is vital to maintaining a strong sense of Self. Seek help from energetic body focused practitioners if you need to learn more about the energy flow of the body.

Family

Love Yourself Through Boundary Setting

Written September 28, 2014

You learn to maintain a strong, healthy, porous boundary to connect in a good way with your inner Self and to interact with others. This chapter includes some boundary setting exercises. I experienced these exercises in various forms at workshops and trainings. Energetic boundaries serve many purposes in our lives. Boundary setting is essential to sever energetic entanglements between the living and the dead. In systemic and family constellations, a long scarf is frequently used to create a physical reminder that there is an energetic separation between the living and the dead, especially when the individual or client is particularly drawn to the dead. We exist in different realms of vibration with some more drawn to the dead than others. It is part of their life journey. The scarf laid out on the floor seems to help those who are energetically drawn to the dead in a strong way find their proper place amongst the living. Quite often these individuals don't seem to be able to find the strength within themselves to create this separation until they visually and viscerally experience the separation as a ritual. I use the word separation, although the reality is that we are always connected. The reason is that in many situations, individuals have lived years, and often many decades, without a healthy boundary around Self. They may have lived since birth in the energy boundary of their mother and in some cases their father. They are familiar with the feeling of energetic entanglement. They feel strange setting up an energy boundary for themselves for the first time. Many clients have to ask what I mean by an energy boundary. They may ask for a description of a boundary before they set about with the task of creating one. If they don't live with an energy boundary, they may live entangled with a parent, or identify with or be attached to the energy field of someone else in the family system such as dead siblings, the ones that died tragically at a young age or those who were miscarried, aborted or stillborn before their own birth; grandparents;

aunts or uncles who experienced trauma; those who commit suicide; the dead in a war on either side; those who experienced tragedy; individuals missing; the victim or the perpetrator; or any other entanglement in the family system.

In one-to-one systemic and family constellations work with clients, I tend to do boundary work with the client prior to setting up a large constellation. I often bring boundary setting activities into the constellation. If the client is emotionally working to release a burden that belongs to other family members or seeking to create a healthy relationship where an unhealthy one currently exists, having the client set up a boundary with a long string of yarn around themselves can be very energetically moving. The client may feel the impact of a boundary at a very deep level. Sometimes it feels liberating and sometimes it feels restrictive. Getting comfortable in the body with an energy boundary is vital. It provides a person with the strength needed to individuate from mother or other family members. Many people find it easy to picture the boundary as an island. Adding some ancestors behind them reinforces a feeling of connection and grounding in the family – a feeling of belonging without having to be entangled. Developing a strong healthy boundary in daily life does take time. It's not magically learned from one boundary activity or one systemic constellation. A constellation can be done in a traditional workshop format and the client leaves with new insight or a new inner image. That fresh image may begin the shift of an unhealthy relationship into a healthy relationship. After a constellation energetically radiates out into the family system, the client may ask, "What's next?" Developing a strong, healthy, porous boundary is next. Boundary setting with the living and boundary setting with the dead. Boundary setting is a key action needed to transform unhealthy relationships into healthy relationships.

In systemic constellations, a representative can be set up for the "Client's Strong Healthy Boundary." In a way, it has some of the same impact as setting up the "Client's Highest Good." However, the difference is that the client takes responsibility for their own wellbeing and it is not left in an abstract form. The client needs to learn boundary setting. It is essential to emotional and energetic wellbeing. Boundary setting is one of the first activities I do with all clients. They need to feel in their body the qualities of their current boundary, or lack thereof, and the issues and challenges associated with it, enabling them to move forward. Boundary practice is essential, and it may need to be reinforced over and over in the future. We have a tendency to slip back into old boundary patterns if we are not careful and present to the way we move forward. Once a constellation is set up, I can make reference to the person's healthy boundary over and over in relation to the relationships set up before them. I can remind them to connect with their healthy boundary and maintain it. In actuality, I am communing with their unconscious mind and the language of their body.

Old habits reinforced through the neuronal pathways of the brain are difficult to shift. Being aware of one's energetic and emotional boundary requires you to be in your body. If you're not in your body, then these old pathways definitely rule the thoughts, responses and actions initiated by your unconscious mind. Boundary setting exercises force you to drop into your body, although, it can sometimes be a long slow process if the individual is in a constant state of emotional numbness or they have a tendency to live energetically outside their body. We have come to understand that emotions are stored in or imprinted on the cells of the body. Many people remain outside their body because the emotional energy in their body is uncomfortable. Unresolved emotional baggage can make life unbearable in the body. All that old emotional trauma and woundedness may have you living outside your body without a boundary, or to the contrary, surrounded with rigid emotional armour, perhaps manifesting as weight gain or the need to be muscle bound. The need for abs of steel may be your emotional armour and your energetic boundary. Others shallow breathe; not realizing it's an unconscious defensive mechanism to keep from feeling energy flow freely through the body. Learning to breathe in oxygen deeply and freely may seem obvious to wellness in life. However, many people rarely experience deep breathing. They often find themselves holding their breath when they are stressed or traumatized by some life event. Accepting your life force energy - the breath of life from your mother - is vital to wellbeing.

Boundary Setting Exercises

Setting boundaries is so important that I decided it was a good idea to write down these activities for others. I didn't create these activities and don't know who did, but I adapted them as an important supplement to my systemic constellation work with others. I live in gratitude to those individuals who did create them. Do you know if you have a strong, healthy, porous boundary or not? Here are some clues for you to consider:

- If you can't say "no" without feeling guilty, you likely lack a strong, healthy, porous boundary;

- If you take care of everyone's needs at the expense of your own needs, you likely lack a strong, healthy, porous boundary;

- If you let others easily into your personal space without any awareness about how that is impacting you, you may not have a strong, healthy, porous boundary;

- If you have difficulty being in relationships with others, you likely lack a strong, healthy, porous boundary;

- If you developed the emotional response of numbness, you likely lack a strong, healthy, porous boundary; and,

- If you stay in your head most of the time intellectualizing, rationalizing and defending, you likely lack a strong, healthy, porous boundary.

A couple of simple ways to get a felt sense of your boundary, or whether you lack one, is to work through the following activities with another person.

Activity 1

Step 1: For the first part of Activity 1, one person will be the Stander and the other will be the Walker. This activity works especially well when people don't know each other well. This may be done as a formal systemic constellation or not. I believe that anytime two or more people meet or work energetically together a systemic constellation has been set up. That means that each of you is physically present, your parents are present energetically and your ancestral lines are present energetically. Begin by facing one another about 40 feet or 12 metres apart. You may have to go outside to do this if you don't have enough space inside. As you face one another at the full distance apart, take a few deep breaths. Take your time to get into your body and be present with your feelings inside.

Step 2: The activity begins with the Stander remaining physically still and present in their body, and to be aware of their feelings inside. The Walker will slowly take a few small steps toward the Stander, pausing after each step is taken. The Stander is to be in touch with what is going on inside their body as the Walker approaches. The Walker can also pay attention to what is going on in their body as they move forward toward the Stander. The Stander pays attention to any anxiety, tightness, tension, elation, desire to push the walker away, or desire to draw the walker in close, etc. and locate where in the body these sensations are felt. The two participants pay attention to thoughts that pop into their minds. They may be reminded of something that happened in the past.

Step 3: The Walker continues to step forward slowly until the Stander feels they want the Walker to stop. The Stander holds up their hand in front like a stop sign to indicate the Walker is to stop. Both the Walker and Stander remain where they are standing. Both the Walker and the Stander make a note of what they felt in this first part of the activity. Could you feel the other person's energy field? As the Walker, could you feel a change within you as you came in close contact with the Stander's energy field? As the Stander, did you feel that you had a strong healthy boundary or was your body willing or calling the Walker to come right into your space, to get closer, or alternatively, did you have a wall of armour up around you wanting to push the Walker away? Did your breathing shift in any way? Do you have a strong healthy boundary in your daily life or do you habitually compromise it? Do you listen to your inner voice and take appropriate actions for yourself or do you ignore it and suffer the consequences of discomfort and tension inside? The Walker may have felt they wanted to stop sooner (perhaps they felt the need for greater space), or the opposite, they may have wanted to walk right up to the Stander and move in close to them (perhaps indicating a lack of boundary or strong inner feelings of abandonment).

Step 4: For the second part of Activity 1, the Walker will take one more step toward the Stander beyond the imaginary stop line. The Stander benefits by paying attention to what is going on within their body when someone violates their boundary. Similarly, the Walker pays attention to what is going on within their body when they violate the boundary of someone else.

Step 5: In daily life, do you require a great deal of space from others or are you comfortable with many people close to you? Who do you allow to get close to you? Who do you keep at a distance? Surprisingly, the answers may indicate either healthy or unhealthy boundaries with others. At the end of the exercise share your experience with the other person. You can switch roles and do the activity again.

Activity 2

Preparation: Cut two pieces of wool or string into twenty-foot or six-metre lengths. Each member of the pair rolls up the wool or string into a small ball and sets it aside. This activity works especially well when people don't know each other well. It is very effective for a facilitator with a new client. However, any two individuals can participate. You may be surprised how frequently pets may join in this activity as many of them naturally love energy work, or maybe they are just tantalized by the long pieces of wool or string. They may willingly help you to test and understand your energy boundaries.

Step 1: Working with your partner, both of you need to sit on the floor on a big cushion, or in a chair if necessary for comfort, about 12 feet or 3 to 4 metres away from each other and facing one another. Ensure that your body is in an open position with arms uncrossed, hanging down by your side. Your legs should not be crossed unless sitting on the floor for comfort. One person will be Person A and one person will be Person B. If handy and available, a third person can guide the activity, or if needed, Person B can guide the activity. Person B will ask Person A to set up a boundary around themselves with the wool and to pay attention to what is going on for themselves as they do it. Person A will slowly use the wool or string to create a boundary around him or herself. Both Person A and Person B take their time and become aware of what is going on inside their bodies as the boundary for Person A is set. Do you begin to feel nervous or anxious? Do you hold your breath or begin to breathe anxiously? Is there any tightening in your body? Where is it located? Is there a temperature change in any part of your body? Is there pressure or tension anywhere in the body? Do any new aches or pains suddenly arise? Do you feel nothing? Does your body go numb as you set a boundary? Notice any thoughts that pop into your mind or other subtle shifts. Do you get all concerned about what shape or size the boundary should be? Do you begin to tap, rock, yawn, laugh or use any other energy escape after you set a boundary? Person B is just watching at this point without a boundary. What does it feel like when one person has a boundary and one person does not? Share your experiences with one another. At this stage, if someone can't feel any sensations, they are likely not in their body. They may be stuck in their head rationalizing the activity. Sometimes we are absent from our body and we don't feel the energy flowing within it. Sometimes we are numb to our feelings and that is our usual emotional response to stress in life. Take notice of all these sensations. If there is numbness, it is important to take some deep breaths of oxygen into the body for this activity so that you can feel the energy flowing. Do something that is grounding to force yourself back into your body. Pause the activity if possible and share a body focused meditation that connects you to different parts of your body, have something to eat or drink, plant your feet firmly on the ground, go out in nature or simply hug a tree for a few minutes. Do whatever works for you. Find your way back into your body and out of your head, even if it feels uncomfortable. Be very aware if you are unable to shift back into your body. If you are not in your body, you will not be aware of your energy boundary. If you are not in your body, this activity may seem pointless to you. Person A shares what they experienced while setting the boundary. What were they feeling and thinking? Was it set with precision or not? Was the size of the boundary considered? Was it a circle or square? Was it open or closed? Was it bigger in the front or the back? Did they want to change it after it was set? Share your experiences with one another.

Step 2: Person B will then take their time setting a boundary around themselves with the wool or string they have. Again, each person is aware of what is going on inside their body when both individuals have a clear boundary. Share your experiences. At this stage, if someone still can't feel any sensations, they are still likely not in their body. It is important for them to bring some oxygen into the body. They may need to take some charged breaths. They need to place their fingertips just under their collarbones and take short gasping inhalations or breaths through the mouth with the mouth hanging open. Touching the upper chest helps a person feel the charged breaths going into that location of their body. Take five charged breaths and see if they begin to feel anything in their body. If there is no impact, take another five and see if they begin to feel energy flowing in their body. If they get dizzy or light headed, they need to stop taking the charged breaths. Getting dizzy is the result of feeling more oxygen then a person is used to handling in their body and they may shift out of their body again to get comfortable. Continue to take in charged breaths until the body can feel the energy flowing within it. Breathe in just enough oxygen to begin feeling sensations in the body. Person A shares their experience of having Person B set a boundary. Is there a comparison of boundary size? Is there a feeling of isolation or abandonment? Does the shape of the boundary seem important? What arises in the body or mind of Person A? Share your experiences.

Step 3: Person B will move forward a short distance toward Person A (a foot or two) and reset their boundary around themselves. Again, each

PATRICIA KATHLEEN ROBERTSON

person is aware of what is going on inside their body when Person B shifts their boundary closer to Person A. Is there any tightening or tension in the body of Person A? Where is the tension located? Does their heart begin to race? Do you find yourself holding your breath? Is your breathing getting shallower? Do you have any aches or pains show up? Does your body temperature change? Do you begin to wish that Person B would move closer? Just notice whatever is going on inside and where you are being impacted in your body. Share your experiences.

Step 4: Repeat Step 3 with Person B moving a bit closer and readjusting their boundary. Person A shares what is going on for them as Person B advances towards them.

Step 5: Repeat Step 3 with Person B moving even closer and readjusting their boundary. Person A shares what is going on for them as Person B advances.

Step 6: Repeat Step 3 with Person B moving forward until their boundary comes close to touching the boundary of Person A, but it isn't touching. Be aware that this may trigger deep emotions in Person A. Person A shares what is going on for them as Person B advances this close.

Step 7: Person B will now move their boundary to just cross over the boundary of Person A. Be aware that this may trigger deep emotions in Person A. How do things shift in the body of Person A? Does this create tension, perhaps creating higher feelings of inundation desiring to push away Person B or to move back from Person B, or does it ease tension, perhaps satisfying higher feelings of abandonment that desire contact, having a desire to draw Person B in closer? Share your experiences.

Step 8: Person B will now move their feet forward out of their own boundary and into the boundary of Person A. Be aware that this may trigger deep emotions in Person A. What is happening in each of your bodies? This activity gives you a strong body-felt sense of your boundary, when it is intact and when it is breeched. Some people do become quite triggered emotionally or agitated at this point in the activity. If possible, sit with this discomfort for a few minutes as it is a great learning opportunity. It is an opportunity to understand your own boundaries more intimately. If you have a significant response, or no response at all, that is how you are energetically interacting with everyone around you as they come close. You may feel like you want someone to come in close, and when they do, you suddenly feel like it is too much energetically, and you may want to push them back. Share your experiences.

Step 9: Person B will now shift back away from Person A in small increments. Share your feelings. Do body symptoms ease for Person A? Is it easier to breathe? Is there a sense of relief? Is there a sense of abandonment? Person A needs to find their healthy distance from others and this is when body symptoms ease. It is important to understand when you are at a healthy distance from others, still able to maintain a strong, healthy, porous boundary. When does the body feel that it is not too close or not too far away? This good distance is found when any anxiety, tension, aches or pains in the body ease. Note the comfortable distance from the other person so that you can take this insight into your daily life and relationships. Person B will then move back one more time. What shifts in the body occur for Person A? Does Person A feel higher abandonment when there is greater distance apart or do they go numb and feel nothing unusual? Does it feel good to have greater distance apart? Share your experiences.

Step 10: Person B will roll up their wool or string. Person B notices how it feels to have no boundary after having had a defined one. Person A notices how it feels to have a boundary when the person you are with doesn't have one. Person A then rolls up their wool or string and notices how it feels to have no boundary. Share your experiences.

Step 11: If time permits, Person A and Person B can now switch places and go through the steps again.

Step 12: Go about your day and be very aware of your boundary with other people. Be aware of when it is okay for others to be closer and when you prefer to have them further away. Be aware what happens in your body if you are in a workplace setting and people just walk in to your workspace unannounced, or they begin to touch things in your workspace without asking for permission first. Be aware what happens as partners, children, parents, siblings or friends step in close to you. How long can you tolerate it comfortably? How close do you let them get? Do you let some in closer than others? Listen to the messages of your body and respond in an appropriate manner. Your body will love you unconditionally for listening to the messages it delivers for your wellbeing. This is all about learning self-soothing activities and engaging in self-care. Can you feel it in your body when another person is too close or too far away? What might you do for yourself to feel comfortable with the person? Do you have to ask the other person to give you more space? Do you need to ask for some alone time? Do you need to ask for more time together? Do you need to take a few deep breaths and then carry on with whatever you were doing? Do you need to move forward slightly or back a bit to help feel good inside and get connected to your boundary? Do you need to go for a walk out in nature to ease a stressful situation or before interacting with others or being fully present? Personal boundary space is a huge element within intercultural interaction. Some cultures tend to routinely engage in closer contact with people than others. Some cultures are more at ease with a hug or kiss on the cheek when meeting, even with strangers. Some cultures are more comfortable touching one another. Some cultures expect distance and formality. Listen to your own body in these situations. Can you shift your boundary to accommodate; yet still actively listen to your own body and put your own needs first? Learning to maintain a healthy boundary is very challenging for some people. Old patterns may continually tempt you.

Step 13: For your own wellbeing, this activity encourages presence in the body. You benefit when you create a life-long habit of body-felt energy awareness and maintain a strong healthy energy boundary for self-care.

These energy boundary activities may help you find your inner Self. The more time you spend in your body the closer you get to your authentic or true Self. You may be in a phase of your life where you find yourself helping others and you neglect your own wellbeing. This is a step on your journey to Self. Be sure to practise having a healthy strong boundary with others. Stay out of agency with others and make it a priority to care for yourself first. When you are ready to stop seeking your emotional wellbeing from the outside world (external referencing), you will find it within (internal referencing). When you maintain a healthy, strong, porous energy boundary, your unconscious mind begins to trust that you will listen to the messages it communicates to you. A strong healthy relationship with your unconscious mind is very rewarding and highly beneficial in living out your soul's purpose. Your unconscious mind, imprinted on the cells of your body, loves it when it can trust that you will listen and respond emotionally in a healthy way. Your unconscious mind will have less need to deliver symptoms and behaviours that seem overly challenging or even frightening.

OCTOBER

Abortion

Written October 20, 2014

This is not a pro-life or pro-choice discussion on abortion. It is not a discussion of the right to have an abortion or not. This is about the emotional and energetic impact of an abortion on the mother and the father, and the greater family system. It's a discussion about what happens when the emotional response to an abortion is silence or indifference, and any heavy emotions felt are suppressed in the body. I look at this topic without blame or judgment; however, I will not address this topic through energetic or emotional blinders.

Systemic Wellbeing

Each person has the right to hold whatever belief system they want around pregnancy and the act of abortion. Abortion is taking the life of your own viable child. To maintain wellbeing over the long-term, a person needs to understand that there are consequences to all actions, including abortion. Each person needs to take responsibility for their own belief systems and those actions; otherwise, someone in the family system may suffer down the road until they do. Taking responsibility means not sweeping emotional responses under the carpet. Taking responsibility means not suppressing emotions in the body. Systemic healing requires a person to take responsibility for their own wellbeing and their own actions. You are asked to evaluate your belief systems to determine whether they serve your highest good, the greater good of your family system and the greater good of humanity. There is a big picture to consider beyond yourself.

Energetic Entanglement

Aborted children often go missing in a family system, which tends to create an imbalance and unwellness in some way. Children missing in the family system may create energetic entanglements with parents, siblings or descendants of the family system until they are acknowledged and emotionally welcomed into the family system by living family members. Every child deserves a place in the family system whether they come to life or not. This includes aborted children, miscarried children, stillborn children, children put up for adoption or put into foster care, and children who die young or tragically. These children deserve to be counted in the family system. Each pregnancy is about new life, about bringing new family members into the world, and each pregnancy counts. They deserve to energetically have a place in their family of origin with their mother and father.

An abortion that is emotionally unresolved and unprocessed may create an energetic entanglement. It may be the beginning of a transgenerational pattern that flows down through the family system until it is resolved. For example, if mother ended the life of one of her children through abortion, her living daughter may lose a child when she gets pregnant. It may become a family pattern for the next generation to lose a child or to struggle to have children until the abortion is acknowledged and emotionally processed. A daughter of the family may feel afraid to have children because she worries she will harm the child, without knowing why. The woman who aborts her child may be drawn to the dead - drawn to her dead child - unconsciously and energetically. She may struggle to be fully emotionally available to her other living children that follow. An abortion frequently creates an exclusion in the family system. Living children who experience being shunned and excluded are sometimes energetically entangled with the aborted child, the one who was excluded from the family system. Living siblings may feel unwanted. They may feel expendable. Living siblings of the child may be drawn to the dead as well. They may feel that something is missing in their lives and they may respond unconsciously with symptoms or addictive behaviours or in some other way. Living siblings may carry survivor's guilt and not understand why. Others excluded by an abortion often include the father of the aborted child and his family system. Many men are unaware they are fathers when an abortion occurs. Whether the creation of a child is consciously known or not, the aborted child may still impact their life in some way energetically. Abortion creates rejection in the family system of the mother and the father. The aborted child is fifty percent mother and fifty percent father. With an abortion, the mother rejects a part of herself and her partner. If the man knows about the child and the abortion, he has also rejected a part of himself and his partner.

Aborted children frequently reveal themselves within the journey of systemic healing. Abortions often show up in the phenomenological approach of systemic and family constellations. A representative of the client may feel out of balance or weak when standing in the family of origin. They may feel that something or someone is missing. Miscarriages, abortions, adoptions, stillbirths or tragedy may create this imbalance or weakness in the family system. It may reveal a child missing in the family system. As with any other action taken by a human being, with an abortion there is an emotional response. The question to explore is whether the emotions were openly expressed and processed by the individuals and/or their family systems, or whether the emotions were left unresolved and suppressed in the bodies of all involved. Suppressed emotion that lingers in the body creates unwellness and it can pass on epigenetically through conception, or prenatally, perinatally and postnatally to your children and grandchildren. For many individuals and family systems the aborted child is never openly acknowledged and/or accepted into the family system. The abortion may be held as a family secret. Systemic healing is about taking responsibility for your conscious and unconscious actions. Is the child welcomed into the family and included when declaring the number of children in the family? Abortion may be a traumatizing situation of death and loss. Was the child appropriately or sufficiently mourned?

Systemic Abortion

I have come to understand that the frequency of abortion is immense and widespread. An emotional and energetic impact may occur in the family system whether there is one abortion or multiple abortions. Abortion impacts all cultures, religious dynamics, ethnicities, social and political realms, and financial strata. Sometimes abortions have been used as a form of birth control when other contraception methods were not available. Sometimes women and men were required by government legislation to restrict the number of children in their family system, such as the One-Child policy in China for several decades. This goes against the natural flow of life. The living siblings of these aborted children may carry heavy guilt. It was their fate to survive and it was the fate of their aborted siblings to die.

Abortion is a complex energetic topic. Recently, during a journey through Eastern Europe, I was told that the average number of abortions for women was very high. The explanation provided was that for many years under communist rule birth control options were limited or non-existent. Many countries did not import contraceptives or provide them openly to the public. In fact, some countries paid women to have more children. Going off on a short tangent, the world witnessed the result of such a law in Romania. Many families were paid to have more children, however, once the children arrived they couldn't afford to support them financially. The extra support promised by the government was limited or short term. Many of these children ended up in orphanages. The emotional neglect within many orphanages, and the early attachment and bonding wounds of these children with their biology mother was immense. As with many adoptions, the early attachment wounds and emotional trauma created lifelong challenges for many of these children, and also for their biological family systems and their adoptive family systems around the world.

In other situations, women that knew they couldn't support the children of many pregnancies, resorted to abortions as a means of birth control. Some women had many abortions. Abortions that are not openly addressed emotionally can create many issues for the partners involved, for other living children of the same partnership, for future partnerships and the offspring of these partnerships, and for future generations. It is fairly common for living children of the family system to struggle in some way. This can lead to the mother, father, and/or their offspring feeling stuck in life in some way unable to reach their full potential or unable to live life fully. They may be drawn energetically and emotionally to a dead child who is missing in the family system. It's important to honestly acknowledge your own emotional response to an abortion so that the systemic healing journey can begin for everyone involved.

Unresolved Blame

If you hold the belief that someone else was to blame for the abortion occurring, that you were forced to have the abortion, or that there is no lingering meaning to the abortion, then you may need to shift that inner image you hold in your body. That belief system may be harming you, your children and your grandchildren physically, emotionally, psychologically, spiritually and relationally. Each woman and man needs to take responsibility for aborting one of their children. In systemic healing, we don't use long, flowing, flowery language when communicating with the unconscious mind. The unconscious mind doesn't respond to complex flowery language. Abortion is taking the life of your own child – it is energetically and physically killing your own viable child. In all bluntness, some consider it murder and feel it should be discussed as such. They feel that to label it any differently is to lighten energetic responsibility. All of these labels and classifications are human constructs. The energetic field is beyond human constructs. Regardless of what it is called, there may be an energetic consequence. The energy around killing your own child reverberates through the family system and through society. You may talk all you want about the viability of the fetus at various stages, and everyone has their right to their own belief system, but the fact remains that an abortion is energetically and physically killing the child that is developing within you. We know that the developing child is gathering information in the cells of their body from the time of conception or even earlier, epigenetically and transgenerationally, through the emotional experiences of their parents and ancestors. A living process is occurring. Abortion is energetically a rejection of yourself and a rejection of your partner. If you have never consciously acknowledged this reality, it might be time that you do. Something amazing may shift within you when you acknowledge and take responsibility for a past abortion. If there are multiple abortions, each one may call for your attention. Think back to the time that the abortion occurred. What was going on in your life at that time? How were you emotionally doing in life at that time? How did the sacrifice of your child's life impact your life? What did the sacrifice of your child's life mean for you? An energetic shift can occur in your family system when abortions are acknowledged and emotionally processed.

System Wide Abortion

Some cultures favour the male child and the result can be thousands, or even millions, of female babies being aborted. Sometimes infanticide occurs after birth and the female child is rejected, neglected and left to die. A few years ago I participated as a representative in a large systemic constellation facilitated in Germany by Bert Hellinger. It revealed the energetic, familial and societal impact of the One-Child policy in China. As the constellation progressed, there ended up being about seventy-five people participating in the constellation. One group represented the unsettled souls of the aborted children. One group represented the keening women in mourning for their aborted children. One group represented the fathers, feeling impotent and helpless to respond to forced or enforced abortion. Systemic healing occurred with the acknowledgement of what is and what was. Healing occurred in honouring those who were aborted – the lives that were sacrificed. It was their fate to die. They were not given the opportunity to come to life. The abortions spiritually, psychologically, emotionally, mentally, physically and relationally impacted the lives of the parents and grandparents, and significantly impacted their siblings that did come to life. Healing occurred when each aborted life was honoured by the living through the intentional commitment to live life fully, to not waste the opportunities that were given through life, to say YES to life as it was given to them, and in letting go of their entanglement with the dead. Some societies are living out the consequences of these aborted children as great imbalances of men and women in communities, especially as it pertains to finding relationship partners.

Energetic Body

A pregnancy is not something that can be energetically reversed. It may be terminated in the physical realm; however, energetically and emotionally there is continuation. There are at least six outcomes for a pregnancy:

- There may be a live single or multiple birth which is full term or premature;

- There may be multiple babies developing in the womb and one or more dies spontaneously;

- There may be a spontaneous abortion or miscarriage;

- There may be an ectopic or tubal pregnancy, with implantation outside the uterus, which usually needs to be terminated because it threatens the woman's life, and the survival of the fetus is rare;

- There may be a stillborn child; or

- There may be an intentional abortion where the life of the child is taken (by force or by choice).

The woman and man who parented the child or children remain parents energetically within their family systems in all these situations. In the situation of abortion, the woman is still a mother and the man is still a father energetically. The aborted child is one of their children and the child needs to be welcomed into the family system. Are there any aborted children missing in your family system?

Intimate Relationship

The abortion effectively ends the intimate partner relationship as it was. As mentioned earlier, since the child holds the energetic and cellular structure of the mother fifty percent and the father fifty percent, the act of abortion has created an energetic rejection of Self and a rejection of the partner. That doesn't mean that the relationship necessarily has to end, although it may. The intimate relationship may continue, however, it may show up in a different way depending on how the abortion was emotionally processed by the woman and the man. With an abortion, there is the death of one relationship as it was known and the birth of a new intimate relationship. Things are never the same as before the abortion. It cannot be the same since the woman is now a mother of a dead child and the man is now a father of a dead child. Especially in situations of multiple miscarriages or spontaneous abortions, the woman and the man are parents together even if no children come to life. The energy dynamic has irreversibly shifted.

Each woman and each man need to acknowledge that they are mothers and fathers from the moment of conception, whether the child comes to life or not. Through pregnancy, the woman and the man created a family system together. Each miscarried child or aborted child is energetically a child of this family system. Each parent of this child is also part of the family system. There are extensive family systems connected to this pregnancy. If you have had numerous miscarriages or abortions, and have no living children, you are still a mother or a father. It is energetically important to own that role in life. The conception of a child tends to create a lifelong energetic entanglement, even if the couple does not remain together. The woman becomes a member of the man's family system and the man becomes a member of the woman's family system. As mentioned earlier, sometimes the father and his family never consciously learn about the child. There doesn't have to be conscious knowledge of this child to have an energetic impact on the whole system. Most relationships that end in pregnancy tend to energetically bring the intimate partners into the family system of the other. A pregnancy may shift even a one-night stand into a significant energetic relationship for life.

Quite often the father of the aborted child is missing from the family system of the mother of the aborted child, and the mother of the aborted child is missing from the family system of the father of the aborted child. The father of the aborted child has a right to belong to the family system. This becomes energetically complex when the pregnancy is the result of an act of violence or sexual abuse. Energetically the father is recognized regardless of whether the child was conceived through love or hate. Using rape as a weapon of war has had a devastating systemic impact in many regions of the world. For many victims, it is unimaginable to welcome a perpetrator into the family system. Sometimes the perpetrator is already recognized as a significant member of the family system in the case of physical or incestuous sexual abuse. I encourage you to read Book 1 of this Series, *Connect With Your Ancestors*, which elaborates on the energetic relationship of the victim and the perpetrator and the energetic dynamics of radical inclusion. Whether the aborted child is excluded, or the father is excluded, the greater collective field doesn't tolerate exclusion. Both the woman and the man need to take responsibility for their actions, acknowledging and accepting what is and what was to move forward in a healthy way in new relationships.

The parents of the aborted child may go on to have new relationships and more children, however, they may struggle with intimacy issues because they are not emotionally available to their new partner. They may not be emotionally available to the children that follow the abortion either. They may be physically present but tend to be emotionally distant or turned away from others close to them. Alternatively, they may be energetically and emotionally overwhelming to their new partner or additional children. They may be drawn to the energy of their dead child or children if the abortion was not emotionally worked through, because the body – the unconscious mind – remembers and seeks systemic healing and balance through these new relationships. Systemic healing is not likely to be found through these relationships. Systemic healing is an inward journey. If the relationship ended with the pregnancy and/or the abortion, another systemic consideration is whether the relationship ended in an honourable way or was it acrimonious? Former partners who were not treated with respect may impact your future relationships and your future children through energetic entanglement. A new partner may feel like they will receive the same treatment from you as you gave your former partner, and they may have difficulty getting close to you. Following an abortion, any children of new relationships may carry the inner fear of rejection, or live rejection continually, and not understand why.

Impact on Siblings

An abortion is the business of the mother and father of the child, not the siblings of the child. However, an unresolved abortion in the family system may impact other siblings in some way. For example, a woman or man may unconsciously yearn for their dead child and be unavailable emotionally to their other children. One of the siblings of the aborted child, or a grandchild in the family system, may be drawn to the dead in some way. They may feel something is missing in their life. Any living children may feel the emotional distance of their parents – parents who are consciously or unconsciously in mourning for their aborted child. Siblings may feel unable to fully take in their own life force energy. They carry the unconscious message in the cells of their body, "I will remember you or I will share this with you." They may be drawn to their dead sibling. Siblings may feel unable to take in nourishment in a healthy way. They may feel out of balance in life or feel that they don't fit well in the family system. They may experience a condition or symptom that seems to linger without responding well to treatment. The struggles of a living sibling may be bringing awareness about the unresolved emotional trauma following an aborted child. It is up to the parents to do their own emotional healing work to welcome the aborted child into the family and to lift the energetic burden from the children that followed the abortion. If they so choose, the parents can tell their living children that they lost a child before they were born, so the living children can feel their rightful birth order.

Emotional Response

What is carried energetically in the body? This may be the body of any family member or the body of the greater family system. Whenever someone is excluded from the family system, an imbalance occurs that seeks to be balanced. There needs to be acknowledgement and acceptance of what is or was. The excluded or forgotten person needs to be welcomed into the family system. What was the emotional response to the abortion? Was the emotional response to the act of abortion sorrow, grief, indifference, pain, shame, guilt, anger, longing, resentment, regret, numbness or some other response? I know some people think about their aborted child or children every day of their lives, whereas, others never admit to consciously looking back. It really doesn't matter what the conscious rational mind does. It is the experience of the unconscious mind - the body - that matters. The contents of the unconscious mind are imprinted on the cells of the body, holding the traumatic emotional cellular memory of the abortion. The body remembers.

Symptoms or Messages of the Body

In the situation of abortion, immune issues may arise if the abortion was never openly and emotionally processed. Immune issues are the body rejecting some aspect of Self, just as the act of abortion is a rejection of Self when understood energetically and systemically. You are encouraged to consider who might be struggling in the family system today as a result of an abortion in the system:

- The mother
- The father
- Siblings of the aborted child
- Later children of the mother
- Later children of the father
- Grandparents of the aborted child
- Grandchildren of the mother or father

Let's review some of the energetic aspects of an abortion. The woman may go on to have other children in life but carry the fear she will harm her children in some way. This fear may be transgenerationally transferred epigenetically to her children while she carries them in the womb. A daughter of the family may carry fear around motherhood or giving birth. She may carry the unconscious or conscious fear of harming her children if she has any, or she may carry the fear that she will be a bad mother. A son of the family may have difficulty committing in relationships because of an unconscious fear of harming his intimate partner, his children or others.

Women of the family may have fertility issues if there is an unresolved abortion in the family system. There may be a child of the family unable to take in their life force energy or nourishment. This includes, but is not limited to, children with eating disorders, children with conditions impacting the digestive system, children with tumours that represent or point to the aborted child, and/or any child that may show symptoms of depression or anxiety for no obvious reason. The child may be drawn to the energy of the dead child creating these symptoms. A child of the family may feel like something is missing in their life. They may unconsciously fear the same fate or fear they will die. Also, many children struggle if they live an inaccurate birth order because a miscarried child or an aborted child is not acknowledged by the family system. Life may feel out of balance or empty without knowing the reason why.

While I was travelling through Eastern Europe, I met one woman who had to wear a cervical neck collar half the time. After a brief discussion, we determined that it might be related to an abortion when she was younger. She had never looked back to acknowledge and heal her unresolved emotional trauma about having the abortion, even though she often thought about the aborted child. This is an example to illustrate how the body manifests the symbolic or metaphoric language of the unconscious mind. How the unconscious mind is the body and the body is the unconscious mind. The neck is meant to turn or swivel the head in each direction – right, left, up, or down – to look at what needs to be seen. Adverse neck symptoms may be a refusal to turn or look back at what needs to be seen, acknowledged, accepted and addressed. A chronic stiff neck may indicate emotional rigidity about some issue. It may indicate that it is time to be more flexible with Self and others, to open one's horizon and to look at the big picture. If you have a stiff neck, don't be afraid to turn your neck to look back at what desires to be seen.

The Aborted Child

In numerous systemic and family constellations, I have witnessed aborted children wanting to be acknowledged, seen and heard by the family system. They energetically want to feel like a welcomed member of the family system. They want their sacrifice to be acknowledged. They want their fate to be honoured. They want to be loved and held in the hearts of their parents. In systemic constellations, the aborted children will often sit on the floor snuggled to their mother's legs. Some of them lie down on the floor with their eyes open, unable to settle calmly into death. Everyone has a right to belong to the family system whether they are alive or deceased. When the sacrifice and fate of the aborted child is honoured and the parents take the child into their heart, then the spirit of the child can be calm in death. Aborted children want any siblings that are drawn to them or drawn to the dead to honour them by living their own lives fully. The living siblings of the aborted child may not know about their dead sibling, so it is up to the mother and father to honour their dead child to benefit their living child(ren).

Mourning the Dead

Abortions, miscarriages, stillborn children, infant deaths, children who die too young, and children who are given away want to be mourned or grieved or remembered in an appropriate and heartfelt manner. In many situations, it is their sacrifice or fate that needs acknowledgement. Frequently, they energetically remain entangled with family members to deliver a message for the balance of the greater family system. If these children were not formally named, or a death ritual or ceremony was not held to honour their life, they tend to be missing from the family system. Even if they were named, they may still be energetically and emotionally impacting current living members of the family system, waiting for an unhealthy relationship to shift into a healthy relationship. Silenced relationships are not healthy. Indifference is not healthy. As mentioned in the previous few chapters on boundary setting, we need to create healthy relationships with the living and the dead. Exclusion creates an unhealthy relationship. There is frequently an unhealthy relationship left unresolved when an abortion has taken place. Living family members may be entangled with family members who are dead, indicating they have unhealthy energy boundaries.

If this is difficult to understand, you might want to think of it as an energetic debt. The life of the aborted child was sacrificed for the mother, the father and the greater familial or societal system. What actions are you going to take to honour that debt or to pay back that debt? What can be done to open the flow of love in the family system where it is currently blocked in this way? Systemically healing this emotional trauma comes in looking back long enough to honestly acknowledge what was and is. Systemic healing comes in sorting out and expressing your feelings and emotions around the abortion. Systemic healing comes in honouring the fate of the aborted child. Systemic healing comes in commemorating the life of the aborted child in some way, perhaps in a meaningful ritual, and welcoming them into the family system. The physical and spiritual demonstration of commemoration will differ for each person, family system, culture or spiritual practice. Energetically, an old inner image held in the body needs to shift. Perhaps it is an image of guilt, indifference or sorrow that needs to shift to acceptance of what is or was. When a life is literally thrown away it needs to be welcomed back into the family system in a heart-felt loving and respectful way. Space needs to be created in the heart for the aborted child to find belonging and peace in death.

The Ritual or Ceremony

Whether you have experienced a spontaneous abortion (miscarriage) or an intentional abortion, there are certain systemic healing actions that can be taken. You may want to sit in a quiet place and light a candle to represent the energy of your aborted child. This place might be in a beautiful setting inside your home or somewhere out in nature. If you don't know for certain, you might want to connect with your body to feel whether the aborted child was a boy or a girl. You might want to picture what the child would look like today and consider what their age would be if they had come to life. You might want to say things to the aborted child that you have always wanted to say, or perhaps take some time to journal your thoughts. You might want to honour the sacrifice the child made so that your life, your family or your society could move forward differently. If there were multiple miscarriages or multiple abortions, light a candle for each child to welcome them into the family system. Do what you can in a meaningful ritual to remember each and every child that did not get a chance to come to life. Take each aborted child into your heart.

Systemic Constellations as Ritual and Ceremony

A systemic constellation ritual or ceremony may be set up to commemorate the life of the aborted child or any miscarried children. It can become a deeply emotional ritual. The family system is set up with markers on the floor to show you, your intimate partner(s) and all your children together, the living and the dead. This constellation sets up the energy of the biological mother and father of a family system. The source of the egg and the source of the sperm that created the developing child in the womb. When there are other family dynamics, such as same gender relationships, these parents can be added to the constellation and placed where it feels right. Begin by setting up the father facing forward, since the sperm of the father fertilizes the seed of life within the mother. The father is set up first because without fertilization by the sperm there is no developing child. Standing in father's position facing forward, mother is set up immediately to his left, and then all the children of the family system are set up to her left going down in age from oldest to youngest in the lineup. Life flows through mother and that is why the children are placed next to her. The constellation can be set up with pieces of paper or pieces of felt or cushions, use whatever is available and meaningful. Take the time to label each piece of paper or marker, perhaps drawing a meaningful symbol on the paper that represents that particular family member. Be sure to remember all the children of the family system. You may want to stand up a book behind each child that did not come to life. This will help differentiate any living children from the dead energetically. The book might represent a grave headstone (please adapt for different cultural and spiritual practices as desired).

Whether this systemic constellation ceremony is for you personally or being set up for a client, place a marker on the floor for each of the miscarried, stillborn and/or aborted children in line with any living children. Have the client feel into their body whether the child was a boy or a girl. This connects them with the energy of the child at a deeper level. This gets them into their body and out of their head. Place a lighted candle on the marker of each family member. If using small tealight candles or votives, it helps to place a small saucer or bowl under each candle to keep from spilling wax everywhere. It also separates the lighted candles from any paper markers for safety reasons. Place the ancestors behind the mother and father in support, include their parents and grandparents. It can be a ceremony for all the children missing from the family system in each generation. You or the client (the mother, father or a grandparent) would then say what they have longed to say to the excluded child or children, and this will vary for each person. You or the client are encouraged to kneel down or sit on the floor in front of each child and to speak in your mother tongue. The mother tongue is the language of the unconscious mind, body, heart and soul. For example, "I am your mother (father or grandparent). You are my child (grandchild). I am willing and able to see you now." "I chose to end your life" (For the grandparent, "Your life was taken, and I was involved in that decision"). "I acknowledge that I took your life to benefit my own. My child (grandchild), I honour your sacrifice and I honour your fate. Now I take you with love into my heart. I give you a place in my heart." This ritual is done for each child missing from the family system. Introduce any living children to their missing siblings. Take time to breathe in this new dynamic energetically and emotionally. Allow any tears to flow to wash out the emotional and physical wounds, to wash away any transgenerational trauma that is flowing down through the family system, and to open the flow of love in the family system. Pay attention to which excluded child draws the greatest emotional response from the client (or Self). This may reveal the most significant energetic entanglement. This is the opportunity to shift the old inner image to a new image, to shift an unhealthy relationship into a healthy relationship. This is the opportunity to take in a new perspective or benefit from new insight. You (or the client) will step upon your own marker in the family system to feel the energy of your complete family system and feel into this strange new sense of balance. Take responsibility for parenting all of the children in the constellation. It is an energetic shift that may initially feel foreign to your body until the emotional wounds feel transformed and systemically healed. Sometimes energetic transformation can be swift and sometimes rituals need to be repeated over and over for the deep unconscious body and soul transformation to occur.

NOVEMBER

Mothers and Daughters (Part 1)

Written November 3, 2014

The relationship between mothers and daughters is energetically, emotionally and spiritually complex on many levels. It is meant to be that way. I write from a place of deep love and respect for all mothers, including my own. I also honour myself as a mother. I write to honour mothers and the role of women systemically. I honour that all women do not become mothers to their own children, however if they don't, they may adopt or foster the children of others, or mother and nurture in other ways. They may be a caregiver, a teacher, a mentor, a coach or a healer to many. They may be a nurturer of animals and pets. They may birth may great ideas into the world.

The relationship with your birth mother set you up with the opportunity to learn all that you wanted to learn during this human lifetime. The relationship with your birth mother provided a catalyst and opportunity for spiritual development and growth. Whether you feel you have a great relationship with your mother or one that is more problematic, there may be opportunities for personal growth and development that you have yet to recognize or explore. By omission, this chapter is not implying that the relationship with father is any less important, however, the intention is to focus on the relationship between mothers and daughters. If you are a son, much of what I have written may be relevant for you too. Feel free to read the chapters on emotional wounds for men and relationships with father in the first book of this series, *Connect With Your Ancestors*. Let me share some systemic healing information about the relationship between mothers and daughters.

Emotional Response Patterns

It is a normal part of early childhood to develop unconscious emotional response strategies and patterns to deal with experiences of emotional trauma and stress. These emotional response strategies and the body holding patterns you develop may remain in place for your entire lifetime, stored in your unconscious mind/body, unless you decide to intentionally shift them. It is up to you as an adult to shift the patterns that no longer serve you well. That's what all this systemic energy healing work is about. What emotional response patterns did you unconsciously develop as a baby and as a young child? Are you the high achiever, the perfectionist, the responsible one, the clingy one, the alien or outsider, the low achiever, the unwanted or undervalued gender of child, the clown, the middle child, the organizer, the take charge one, the abandoned one, the black sheep, the invisible one, the worker, the nurturer, the stubborn one, the entertainer, the quiet one, the hero or rescuer, the one left out, the protector, the fragmented one, the fixer, the helper, the psychic one, the invisible one, the sensitive one, the procrastinator, the martyr, the indecisive one, the know-it-all, the weak one needing protection, the irresponsible one, the victim, the sickly one, or the one focused on outer physical appearance or material wealth? Maybe you identify in another way. What about birth order? Are you the oldest or the first born after a long gap in the family? Do you carry the middle child syndrome? Are you the baby of the family? How many older children are between you and the attention of your mother? Do you feel like there is a sibling missing in your family of origin? You might want to look to your life, interests and career choices to help you sort out your early emotional response patterns. You may carry a combination of several of these emotional response strategies, or many others from a long list. The development of these emotional response patterns was your means of emotional survival as a baby in and out of the womb, and throughout childhood.

The Psyche

When the energetic and emotional connection with mother weakens for a daughter, or an attachment wound forms, she may respond emotionally in a number of ways. The child may take on the energy pattern of: I'm not good enough. I'm alone. I don't matter. I'm inadequate. I'm unworthy.

I'm rejected. I will die. I'm not safe. I don't fit. I don't deserve to live. I don't exist. I'm a failure. I'm ugly. I'm left out. I'm separate. I'll lose control. I'm not lovable. I'm an embarrassment. I'm not wanted. I'm not important. I'm not loved. I'm responsible. I need to be perfect. I don't need anyone. The daughter holds this pattern, or perhaps several emotional response patterns, in her body for life unless body focused energy work is embraced to transform the pattern. These patterns may have been your way of being seen by your mother or your way of showing up in your greater family system. Mother may have been very busy with many other children in the home or she may have had a great deal of work to do, and you may have felt emotionally abandoned or threatened or not seen. Sometimes this happens even if you are the only child and mother was emotionally distant and drawn energetically to something emotionally unresolved that occurred in her past. Each child of the family system will respond differently to mother emotionally. Remember that an only child may carry the emotional wounds from both mother's and father's family systems.

The Biology

Let's go back to the beginning to explore the development of your emotional response strategies. The young child develops these emotional response patterns to survive at all costs and to overcome feelings of annihilation or extinction. These emotional response patterns are biological, evolutionary survival mechanisms built into the baby's body. That is why the biology or physiology of the body cannot be separated, diagnosed or studied separate from the emotional dynamic of the human being. Emotional unwellness brings on physical, psychological, spiritual, mental, relational and financial unwellness.

An attachment or bonding wound may have developed with mother even if something huge, obvious or seemingly significant did not occur. If you are an adult or child, behind that diagnosis of cancer you may be carrying familial and ancestral emotional woundedness. Behind that heart disease may be an ancestral broken heart. Behind those digestive issues may be an ancestral emotional inability to take in nourishment or starvation. Behind the addictions may be an inability to settle into the energy of the body because of the feelings of heavy ancestral emotional pain or trauma.

The measure of life stress or trauma is subjective and individual to each one of us. It is contextual. You may be able to handle an emotional dynamic in one situation, but struggle with it in another situation or at a different time in your life. What may appear insignificant to one person may be felt intensely by another. That is why many quantitative, empirical studies omit important aspects of the human condition. Emotions are part of the biology. Emotions are imprinted on the cells of the body. They cannot be ignored. They are not separate. They cannot be studied separately. These unconscious emotional events in relationship with mother set your inner fears in place for life. Fear is interconnected with your emotional response strategies and it is a complex emotional state that definitely creates unwellness and imbalance if it is allowed to take over your life. To release or reduce fears, worries and grief is all part of a systemic healing journey.

The Pregnancy

Was your mother's pregnancy with you welcomed with love or was your mother horrified to discover she was pregnant? Did your mother struggle emotionally in any way while she was pregnant with you? Was your mother well supported during her pregnancy by your father and her family members, or was there conflict or uncertainty of some sort going on in her life? Regardless of your birth situation, you all have a mother and a father, even if father was a sperm donation. That sperm is connected to an entire family system that cannot be ignored. Take the time to understand the impact of your mother's pregnancy scenario on your life today. The baby developing in the womb may feel any adverse emotional state of her mother and feel it as a threat to her life. The baby takes the emotional experience and emotional memory of mother epigenetically into the cells of her body moment-by-moment, hour-by-hour, and day-by-day. With a full-term pregnancy, there are about nine months' worth of emotional experiences to consider. The baby's primary goal at this point in life is survival and she will respond accordingly. If the baby feels mother as emotionally unwell or needy, the baby may unconsciously offer to take care of mother's emotional wellbeing from that moment onward. The baby unconsciously sacrifices her own wellbeing out of love and loyalty to the greater family system to come to the emotional aid of her mother. The child develops emotional strategies in agency with mother in order to ensure survival. The baby unconsciously says, "your needs will come before my needs mother." This process occurs for all babies in one way or another and to varying degrees, with diverse emotional outcomes.

The felt sensation in the body of the baby becomes, "If mother is doing okay, I will survive." As a little baby coming into the world you may have taken on the body-felt sense, "I have to comfort her and carry her pain. She can't do it on her own. She isn't strong enough emotionally." "I am responsible for her wellbeing. She won't be happy and fulfilled if I don't carry or at least share her emotional burden." "I have to take care of things and do a good job, or I won't survive." "I need to fix things for mother." That is the unconscious emotional life of the developing baby. At this very early moment of life, to ensure survival, the daughter sacrifices herself, and she becomes a martyr to carry or share mother's emotion pain. At that moment, the daughter sets herself up for a lifetime of struggle. She will suffer. She feels like a failure in each life experience. Carrying the emotional burdens of mother is far too much for any child. That unconscious decision may set up the child for the journey she wanted to experience in this lifetime, for development emotionally, and for the opportunity to develop other skills and talents she wanted to acquire. When you carry these early emotional response patterns into adulthood, each adverse situation that you face feels once again like a situation of survival. That makes it very difficult to be in relationship with others and explains why so many relationships are challenging and why so many of them tend to end. Remember that all relationships are not meant to be forever. Some relationships are meant to be for a short period of learning in your lifetime. These early emotional response strategies help to explain the relationships that develop between mothers and daughters. These same dynamics may pertain to sons and their mothers as well.

The Birth

What did you experience at birth? You were suddenly delivered into this strange and frightening new world leaving behind the warmth of mother's protective womb. Was your mother there to greet you physically at the time of your birth or was she drugged? Was your mother there to greet you emotionally or was she overwhelmed with her own trauma and early childhood issues, perhaps triggered emotionally by pregnancy and the birthing experience? It's a reflexive autonomic action for the survival of the baby to bond with mother. You searched for the warmth of mother's body against yours, you looked up into mother's eyes to make a connection and to feel welcomed, you searched for a nipple to nourish and comfort you, and you searched for confirmation that life outside the womb was a good experience. Perhaps mother breastfed you and perhaps she didn't. You may or may not have breathed in your full life force energy, your birthright from your mother.

Many come through the birth process to life and mother is not present emotionally or energetically. There may have been birth complications and mother's energies were scattered. Maybe your life was at risk and emergency intervention was required. Maybe you were whisked off to a nursery to be cared for by strangers. Maybe your survival meant being placed in an incubator. Maybe your birth triggered mother's own childhood wounds. Maybe her birth was traumatic and she carried fears around birthing that were held by her mother. She may have been overwhelmed with feelings of unresolved emotional childhood or ancestral wounds or trauma and turned away energetically. Perhaps, from her place of emotional woundedness, mother experienced your birth as her source of love and her source of comfort. Rather than giving to you, which is the natural flow of life, mother

STEP INTO THE LIGHT

energetically received or took from you. You unconsciously sacrificed your own wellbeing and became the giver to mother, and this has followed you throughout life.

Mother's Emotional World

Mother was there physically, however, emotionally and energetically she was absent. There are many dynamics that set this up. Mother may have been drawn energetically by any unresolved emotional trauma in her family system such as when a child in the family died young, was miscarried, aborted or stillborn, or was given up to adoption; a parent leaving or dying young; a lost or unrequited first love; accidents and other tragedies; deep family secrets that were left unresolved; the experience of war, conflict, violence, displacement, religious persecution or political oppression; or someone might be missing or excluded from her family system.

Do your best to create an understanding of mother's emotional childhood experience. You will have to step outside the box for this activity. If you stay within your narrow perception of childhood and remember only the worst dozen things your mother did, you may not be able to imagine the situation that existed for your mother and you as a baby or child. You may be unable to tap into all that your mother did do well for you energetically. You may not be able to get acquainted with your mother at a deeper level. You may not be able to have compassion for mother and understand that she did the best she could for you considering what was passed to her emotionally as a child, or she experienced as an adolescent or adult. Here are some questions to consider:

- Who was your mother when she was a child?
- Who loved your mother when she was a child?
- What were your mother's dreams?
- Who supported your mother's dreams?
- What do you know about your mother's parents?
- What did your mother's parents emotionally pass to her?

103

- Did your mother have siblings?

- What do you know about your mother's siblings?

- Did your mother's siblings (if she had any) do well in life?

- What emotional trauma occurred in your mother's life (may have been in the womb)?

- How did any trauma impact your mother's life?

- Did your mother have many friends when she was a child or adolescent?

- Did your mother like school (yes or no), and if not, why not?

- If she liked school, what was your mother's favourite subject?

- What did your mother like to do with her spare time as a child and adolescent?

- What were your mother's natural gifts and talents?

- What was going on in your mother's community when she was growing up?

- What was going on around the world when your mother was a child or adolescent?

- What do you know about your mother's grandparents?

- Did your mother emigrate? If she didn't, who in the family did? If she did, did she continue to speak her mother tongue?

The list of questions is endless. If your mother is alive, take the time to ask her every question that comes to mind. It is important to show your mother that you care about her life, not just your own. This activity can be life changing for you and your mother. Be aware that the unresolved emotionally traumatic events held within your mother's body might have occurred in her generation or in past generations. Once you have asked your mother all the questions that seem important to you, if your father is alive and available, ask him all the same questions. If your mother and father are no longer alive, ask other extended family members about the lives of your parents as children, or do research to recreate it yourself for the time period where they grew up.

Separation Wounds

A daughter's relationship with her mother becomes the template or blueprint for all her future relationships. If the relationship went reasonably well, the daughter likely feels confident, loved, and has high self-esteem and self-worth. When you are honest with yourself, do you feel that you got enough energetically and emotionally from your mother? Are you still seeking something from your mother? This question is asked without any blame or judgement. It is meant to acknowledge what is or was. Ponder your current situation; do you rely on others to keep you feeling safe in the world? Perhaps you have a tendency to feel insecure or struggle with uncertainty. Perhaps you feel unsafe in life or in relationships. You might find you have a tendency to want to control things in life to feel safe. You might need structure in your life to feel safe. You might dislike change because it generates feelings that are underpinned by a lack of safety. Looking at other examples, you might have difficulty with intimacy because it generates feelings of betrayal. You may not have a strong sense of self-worth or self-esteem, or you may lack confidence. You may not feel loved or wanted. Many of these feelings developed in relationship with your birth mother. If you are a resilient survivor, those feelings also developed in relationship with your birth mother. Are you able to love yourself unconditionally or do you seek love from others to feel good about yourself? This emotional pattern developed in relationship with your mother.

If mother wasn't fully present emotionally, energetically, spiritually or physically for you, a relationship of emotional distance may have established. There is no blame or judgement here. Mother may have been overwhelmed with the trauma experienced in her childhood, and these events or situations can be very subtle yet greatly impactful, and the transgenerational trauma she carried for her family system. You may have experienced an early emotional attachment wound or bonding wound with mother. Your emotional response pattern may be independence. "I don't need anyone." "I'm just fine on my own." "I made it on my own." "Once I left my childhood home I never took anything from my parents again." Hyper-independence does not help you have healthy relationships in adulthood. You might have found one person in your life that you could really trust, and you became quite dependent on them. Your lives became interwoven together in co-dependence. Quite often you don't recognize your own emotional response patterns until you have lived a few decades and experienced many of the same repetitive relationship patterns over and over.

Not Enough of Mother

If you experienced an emotional attachment wound with mother, it may create an energy dynamic of abandonment that will impact your life in a huge way. A daughter that feels she didn't get enough from mother may have abandonment issues. Each time the daughter gets close to someone she may develop the same inner feeling she experienced with mother. If the daughter experienced energetic abandonment, in a close relationship with family, friends or an intimate partner, the daughter may want to draw people in close to her. However, if they get too close to her energetically, or stay around too long, she may unconsciously push them away. She didn't experience closeness with mother, so she may have difficulty experiencing closeness with others. This woman may be drawn to live her old familiar pattern of abandonment. She actually creates this dynamic herself, yet, convinces herself that everyone else can't get close.

Too Much of Mother

If the relationship with mother was energetically overwhelming, the daughter may push her mother away. This often happens in adolescence. It is the time in a girl's life, around puberty, when she is meant to connect with the strong circle of women in her family system, her mother and all the many grandmothers behind her. The daughter who pushes away her mother may struggle at some time in life physically, emotionally, psychologically, spiritually, financially, or as mentioned, with regard to relationships. Often, a daughter will feel emotional distance from her mother, blaming mother for this distance, when the reality is that the daughter unconsciously rejected mother and placed distance between them. Sometimes the daughter is too close to the father and that makes it difficult to get close to mother (daddy's girl). If the daughter experienced energetic inundation (flooding) as a child and adolescent, she may initially push others away. This includes a daughter still entangled in her mother's energy boundary, a daughter who is mother's confidante or a daughter of a helicopter parent. If these feelings persist, she eventually begins to feel out of balance, unwell or perhaps lonely. Often in desperation, her response may be to eventually gather someone to her so that she can experience the energetic inundation she felt in childhood. That is her comfort zone. She may feel alone even when others are present and too much time with others may set up the desire to send them out the door. If you don't work to minimize the impact of the relationship style you developed early in life, you may fall back to the default position of abandonment or inundation that you experienced as a child, likely bouncing back and forth between the two.

Bonding Wound

A bonding or attachment wound with mother at birth or in early childhood may create an energetic entanglement with mother. For example, if your birth experience wasn't particularly welcoming, if your mother had to be in the hospital for a time when you were young or if another sibling arrived when you were at a very young age, it may have triggered an attachment wound with mother. If mother went to work when you were young, or she went off on a vacation without her child(ren), an attachment wound may have developed. If you were sent to live at the home of an extended family member or with others outside the family for periods of time at a young age, an attachment wound may have developed. Adoption at birth or at an early age immediately creates an attachment wound with mother.

It is my belief that the development of an attachment wound with mother is to some extent unavoidable, since mothers are only human after all, and mothers cannot satisfy every desire or need of the baby or child. It seems to me these attachment wounds are a necessary part of our human journey on planet Earth as spiritual beings. I believe that attachment wounds with mother are part of the human condition. They are certainly not pathological, except under extreme situations. These attachment or bonding wounds can certainly be transformed and systemically healed.

An emotional response pattern that created emotional distance from mother may bring about a rejection of mother and/or a merging with mother. A daughter may consciously or unconsciously attempt to be the opposite of her mother, hence rejecting her, or she may unconsciously take on many of mother's qualities, merging with her. What you reject in your mother you also reject in yourself, since you are genetically fifty percent mother. If you have been seeking wellness for decades, and yet it seems elusive, it is important to understand that you cannot get connected to your authentic inner Self within and a feeling of unconditional love for yourself if you consciously or unconsciously reject your mother. Regardless of what your mother may have done or not done, you cannot consciously or unconsciously reject your mother and expect to find self-love and balance. You may find you carry a thick layer of rigid energetic armour or draw upon physical weight or extreme muscle to protect your inner Self and to guard against emotional pain. Through participation in many systemic and family constellations around chronic illness, it is often found that rejection of mother can contribute to many immune system conditions. Contrarily, if you have merged with mother, you may not have a strong healthy energetic boundary of your own and this is a key area of systemic healing work for you. You may still be energetically and unconsciously in your mother's energy boundary caring for her emotional needs. You may consciously or unconsciously feel inside that your mother is not strong enough to carry her own fate or burdens in life. This can be a major stumbling block for many daughters – feeling bigger than or superior to their mothers (and/or their grandmothers). This detrimental inner image held in the body will need to shift for relationships to be healthy in life.

Relationship with Mother

At times, I've heard it said that the way you respond to group situations is the way you feel in relationship with your mother or how you experienced your mother. It is another way to evaluate your energy boundaries. How do you emotionally respond to group settings?

- Are you overwhelmed by groups?

- Do you feel responsible for everyone's comfort in a group setting?

- Do you lack confidence in a group?

- Do you dread being in groups?

- Do you feel threatened in groups?

- Do you stand on the margin in a group setting?

- Do you feel like it is your role to make everyone happy in a group?

- Do you thrive in a group setting?

- Are you quiet in group settings?

- Do you shrink energetically in a group of people?

- Do you become the busy worker behind the scenes within a group?

- Do you make yourself indispensable in a group?

- Do you immediately step in to take charge and organize things in a group, to become the leader?

- Do you attempt to stand out or be noticed by the group, the centre of attention?

These questions and their answers might be something to ponder to help you sort out your relationship with your mother. The answers may help you understand any early childhood attachment or bonding wounds you may have experienced and childhood emotional response strategies you may carry that continue to impact your life today.

Family

Mothers and Daughters (Part 2)

Written November 12, 2014

Is the relationship with your mother problematic? Perhaps your mother has passed to the other side and you have some lingering regret or anger? Please know that it is never too late to shift the inner image you hold of your mother. This is not about creating a fairy tale about your relationship. It's about looking back at the big picture. The daughter leaves childhood with a narrow view of her mother. In her eyes, she remembers the dozen things her mother didn't do well. The daughter doesn't integrate all the things her mother did right to bring her to adulthood. The daughter isn't usually focused on the greater systems surrounding her mother. The child is usually the central focus of her own life. The daughter often does not have knowledge of the trauma in her mother's background and the impact it had in her life. Shifting the relationship you have with your mother means developing compassion for the journey mother had through her childhood and life, or to acknowledge the transgenerational trauma she shares or carries for her family system out of unconscious love and loyalty. What emotional response patterns did your mother develop in her childhood to survive or tolerate the emotional environment around her? What emotional patterns did your grandparents and great grandparents pass down to your mother? What events or situations happened in mother's life before you came along? In the last chapter we reviewed your mother's early life. How much did you know about it? You need to remember that mother could only be emotionally what she learned and absorbed from others, unless she worked through much of her unresolved trauma and learned adult emotional response patterns. I have discovered that in most family systems that is not highly likely. You also need to understand what mother carried epigenetically for her family system. The knowledge and resources to address mother's emotional response patterns and the transgenerational trauma she carried were not readily available in the past. Also, it's really only the last few generations that have had the time for much self-reflection.

That leaves you, the daughter, to shift things today. Remember to look back without blame and judgement.

Did mother or her ancestors experience emotional trauma that was left unresolved or repressed in the family system? This unresolved emotional trauma would have been stored in the cells of your mother's body. It would have been passed down to her children, you and your siblings if you have any. Is there a pattern of emotional distancing in the family system? Are emotional events silenced? It is a great time to ponder what can be done if there is an unhealthy emotional relationship with mother or a poor inner image of her. One key aspect that seems to show up continually in systemic and family constellation work is that daughters seem to be able to engage in life and relationships more successfully when they are solidly positioned in their mother's circle of energy, not her energy boundary, in a healthy way by around the time of puberty. It seems to help if women are able to feel the support of the long line of strong women in their family system behind them. A daughter of the family system needs to develop a strong understanding that the women of each generation did the best they could for their family with the life experiences they incurred and the physical and emotional resources that were available to them.

Individuation

I would like to clarify that there is a major difference between a "circle of energy" and an "energy boundary." Being in mother's circle of energy is not the same as remaining in mother's energy boundary. The two are very different. To be a teenaged daughter in your mother's circle of energy is a good thing, however, to be a teenaged daughter still in your mother's energy boundary is not a good thing. Let me explain the difference.

Circle of Energy

In the journey through early childhood, a daughter is hopefully in the process of beginning to individuate from mother by about three or four years old. The hippocampus of the child's brain is more fully developed for the functions of memory and emotions at that time. The child is less biologically dependent on mother for survival. The child is more open to relationships with others. The child slowly moves away from mother to explore the world beyond her. The child begins to feel okay playing away from mother, perhaps going to a playschool or preschool for a few hours each day. Perhaps the child feels okay playing for a while at the home of a friend.

If this individuation process moves in the right direction, the daughter develops her own healthy energy boundary. She will be able to sense her own inner wellbeing separate from her relationship with mother and relationships with others. She will connect to her inner Self to feel her wellbeing. She no longer needs to look to others to know if she is doing well. This process of individuation continues throughout childhood, adolescence and adulthood as the daughter relies less and less on mother and others to understand and feel her own wellbeing. When the woman is triggered emotionally by some event, or the words or actions of another person, she doesn't feel threatened like she did as a child. She doesn't need to be defensive since she knows her worth inside. She doesn't need to rationalize over and over in her head. She doesn't need to look to others to help her feel safe in the world. She finds safety within. She connects to her inner Self to find wellbeing, to soothe herself, to self-parent when she feels she didn't get enough from mother and/or father, and to give unconditional love to herself. The woman who is connected to her authentic inner Self feels connected in a healthy way to the greater systems around her.

Energy Boundary

To be positioned in mother's energy boundary long past childhood is problematic and it happens to many people. If you leave childhood and still expect something from your mother and father, you are likely energetically entangled with them. Earlier in this book, there were several chapters written about the significance of individuals developing a healthy energy boundary with Self and others. If you are still in your mother's energy boundary as an adult, consciously or unconsciously caring for her emotional needs, and entangled with her emotional burdens in life, you may struggle in life one way or another. The daughter may struggle to individuate from her mother. The energy of mother draws the daughter back to her continually. As a baby or child, the daughter may have unconsciously sacrificed her own wellbeing for the wellbeing of her mother. The baby may have felt like her survival was threatened at times, so she voluntarily and unconsciously, out of love and loyalty, took on the job of caring energetically and emotionally for mother. Later, as the daughter attempts to individuate, she unconsciously feels guilty if she leaves her mother. In relationships, she may unconsciously feel that she is betraying her mother if she gets too close to others. Emotional wellbeing requires you to separate from mother's energy boundary and develop your own healthy energy boundary with Self and others. To have physical, emotional, spiritual, psychological, financial, mental and relational wellbeing as an adult, you need to have a strong healthy relationship with your deep inner Self. This is the foundation for having a healthy energy boundary with others. The energetic distance between the daughter and her mother in a healthy relationship is the love between them without the entanglements.

Mother Unable to Let Go

Mother may have trouble letting her daughter leave her energy boundary. Mother feels lonely when her daughter moves away from her side. Mother's early attachment wounds or bonding injuries with her mother (grandmother) as a baby and young child rear their head. Perhaps grandmother had many children and mother was well down the line energetically a long distance from her mother, and emotionally she didn't feel like she got enough. Perhaps grandmother lost a child before mother was born and grandmother was drawn emotionally to the dead child. Alternatively, if mother was emotionally and energetically sensitive, she may have drawn to her dead sibling. Regardless of the underlying trauma, mother feels abandoned when her daughter moves out of her energy boundary. Mother may feel alone or vulnerable. Mother may unconsciously feel betrayed and not understand why. Mother doesn't consciously realize that her daughter is taking care of her emotional needs. The daughter is living in agency with her mother and this is energy deadening for the daughter. Mother feels off balance as the daughter moves away emotionally and energetically. Mother may emotionally collapse when her daughter goes off to college or university in another city. Mother struggles when the nest is empty. When the daughter cares for her mother's emotional needs and carries or shares her burdens, both the mother and daughter may be weakened energetically.

Mother unconsciously projects her own fears and emotional trauma onto her daughter. Mother draws her daughter back to her over and over. Mother is unable to sever the energetic umbilical cord with her child. This creates an unhealthy relationship between mother and daughter. Remember that a close relationship with mother is not always a healthy relationship with mother. For example, a daughter that is mother's best friend or mother's confidante in life is not likely in a healthy relationship with her mother. This process of individuation from mother is relevant for daughters and sons. To attain healthy individuation in life, it means you need to pass mother's emotional burdens back to her, since she is the rightful energetic owner of them. As the daughter, you need to feel deep in your body that mother can carry her own emotional burdens in life. If you experience your mother as weak emotionally, you may not be able to energetically pass the emotional burdens back to her. Each of us is stronger when we live our own fate and carry our own emotional burdens, no matter how difficult the burdens may seem. Mother is felt as weaker because you have been sharing or caring her unresolved emotional burdens. You have been too big energetically. A daughter suffers when she is too big energetically. In a systemic or family constellation laid out before you, it is emotionally helpful to experience mother with a system of support behind her such as her parents, grandparents or the long line of women in her maternal family line. As the daughter, you may gain energetic strength in connecting to the long line of women in your family system.

Living in Agency with Mother

Some children feel like they were born to take care of their mother. They often don't realize this until they are adults themselves. I have written about babies and children unconsciously sacrificing themselves out of love and loyalty for the wellbeing of the greater family system. If the developing baby feels mother's emotional energy as needing support, the baby may unconsciously offer to share or carry mother's unresolved emotional issues. This dynamic continues until you acknowledge that it exists consciously, and then do some systemic healing work to shift it. If you are carrying mother's emotional trauma, you may also be carrying maternal grand-mother's emotional trauma. The three-generational impact is important to consider here. While maternal grandmother was carrying her daugh-ter (your mother) in the womb, did any emotional event or trauma occur to impact grandmother? Was grandmother well supported by her partner and her family during her pregnancy? Did grandmother live through a war carrying fear for your mother's safety and wellbeing? What was happening in the region of the world where grandmother lived during that period of time? One emotional trauma might impact grandmother, mother and you, since you are one of the eggs present in the ovary of the developing baby (mother) by the time she is at the five-month gestational point in the womb of grandmother. These emotional impacts can have a huge effect on a family system over many generations epigenetically and they can remain a mystery to everyone involved. Please don't underestimate their transgen-erational impact.

Too Much of Mother

Learning about systemic healing requires a back and forth approach (an iterative approach). Some concepts and ideas are visited many times in many ways. You will find this is an extension of the last chap-ter. Sometimes mothers are emotionally distant, yet physically present. Mother may be overly present. Mothers may overwhelm their children energetically because of their own inner woundedness. A daughter may feel overwhelmed by mother's energy being too much or too overpowering all the time. A daughter living in her mother's energy boundary may feel overwhelmed by mother's energy. A daughter may find she is expected to live out all mother's unfulfilled dreams. A daughter may energetically struggle to exist or to be seen for who she really is inside. She may struggle to live her own destiny or have no idea what that might be. A daughter may unconsciously attempt to push her mother away. It might involve physically moving away to a distant location. This may or may not show up in her physical behaviour. It may be an internal feeling of pushing away. It may be mirrored later in relationships. A partner will get close and the woman will push him or her away. She may need a lot of space in relationships. It feels energetically like too much when the partner gets close, just like the relationship with mother. Systemic healing requires the daughter to acknowledge and understand her inner struggles and her own suffering within the big picture of the family system.

Helicopter Parents

Helicopter parents were mentioned in a prior chapter. If you recognize yourselves here, you tend to live this dynamic with one or more of your children. Helicopter parents are the ones who show up on university campuses, arguing with professors to get the "A" grade they feel their adult child deserves. Helicopter parents take care of life for their adult children and often attempt to control their lives. Helicopter parents might enjoy having their adult children live at home long after it is time for them to move out on their own. This is different than a cultural practice of multi-generational households, although it might still be relevant in some situations. Helicopter parents are afraid to let go. They are afraid to let their children learn through failure or making mistakes. It would be interesting to do a study on helicopter parents. I wonder how many helicopter parents experienced emotional distancing or hands-off parenting in their childhoods? Their emotional response may be to overcompensate and inundate their child emotionally, perhaps to do the opposite of their parents. This reveals a rejection of the prior generation and subsequently a rejection of Self.

Not Enough of Mother

Again, this is an extension of the last chapter. When a woman feels like she didn't get enough emotionally and energetically from mother, she may merge with mother or judge mother. In judging mother, she rejects mother as she is or was. In rejecting mother, she may also merge with mother. If you intentionally attempt to do things the opposite to your mother, you have energetically rejected her. This daughter may turn around and overwhelm her children energetically. In responding from her own inner woundedness, she may overcompensate. She overwhelms her children energetically. In being too much or too close energetically for her children, the children may eventually turn around and respond the opposite with their children, if they have any. These inundated children may give less energetically and be less present emotionally for their children. A family pattern may develop where the generations begin to flip back and forth from abandonment to inundation and then back to abandonment again in a repetitive cycle.

Rejecting Mother

If a daughter leaves childhood blaming her mother for anything, stemming from feelings of energetic abandonment or inundation, an unhealthy relationship exists that needs to be addressed for emotional wellbeing as an adult. Sometimes the daughter may feel like something isn't right in life, however, she isn't consciously able to put her finger on the issue or to name it. She just feels stuck in life in some way. Life feels incomplete even when she has everything she needs in a material sense. She may continually struggle in life in relationships or with employment situations. The daughter may have consciously or unconsciously rejected her mother and/or merged with mother. In rejecting her mother, she may take on some of her mother's less favourable characteristics and qualities. This is how the daughter unconsciously or subversively shows her love to her mother, or how she remains energetically connected to her mother, if there is physical or emotional estrangement. As the daughter ages, she may feel like she is becoming her mother. It's important to understand that the feelings of abandonment or inundation are part of human development and they are not pathological. However, they do influence life in a huge way until you learn to minimize or reduce their impact.

Life Force Energy

There are many emotional response patterns developed early in life. When the daughter has an attachment or bonding wound with mother, as discussed in Mothers and Daughters (Part 1), she may not feel worthy or deserving of taking up space in the world. She may not have a healthy energy boundary of her own. She may be without a boundary, or conversely, she may have built up rigid energetic armour to guard her heart and her deep inner Self. This daughter may have difficulty breathing in her full life force energy. She may not be able to take in nourishment in a healthy way. She may be a shallow breather or a person who regularly holds her breath when life gets challenging. She may not be able to take in deep healthy breaths of oxygen. She may withdraw or pull away when relationships run into conflict or obstacles.

Mommy's or Daddy's Girl

A daughter may struggle to commit fully in relationships if her heart belongs to mommy or daddy. She may unconsciously feel guilty if she gives her heart to another. She may struggle to create intimacy in relationships. She may feel like she is betraying her mother or father if she enjoys a sexual relationship with an intimate partner. If mommy and/or daddy are placed high on a pedestal above reproach, the daughter may find constant fault in her partner. The partner may struggle to live up to the expectations of the woman. Mommy is the child's first love, and daddy, the daughter's first love of the opposite gender, even if the relationships are far from ideal.

These dynamics will be different in same gender family systems. When the child grows up and enters relationships, she may struggle with same or opposite gender relationships, depending on the unresolved emotional and energetic dynamics she experienced in her family system. The family of origin relationships are a template for how to be, or how not to be, in future relationships with others. To find success and happiness in relationships as an adult, the daughter may need to separate herself from these energetic entanglements with mother and father. To find success as a woman and become emotionally mature, a young girl needs to be firmly planted in her mother's circle of energy, not mother's energy boundary, with all her long line of strong, effective women ancestors that did the best they could for their families. There were women in the family line that got it right or else the family line would have ended generations earlier. When a woman doesn't have a healthy relationship with her mother, she needs to make her way back to her mother's circle of energy - both energetically and emotionally – if not in the material world – then with the spiritual realm. This journey back requires you to explore the past, to acknowledge what was without blame or judgement, and to develop compassion for the life journey of mother, regardless of how well you thought she did in her role. This is how you shift the inner image you carry about your mother. It's not about making up a new story or creating a new narrative in your head. It's about acknowledging the greater systemic reality of the past as you expand to take in the big picture view of your family system and your family members. It's about finding your family's place within your greater community and in the broad universe beyond.

DECEMBER

Mothers and Daughters (Part 3)

Written December 4, 2014

Your mother was the perfect mother for you!

What is your immediate emotional response to that statement? The answer that comes without thought, defensiveness, rationalizing or intellectualizing will reveal much about where you are along your emotional and spiritual healing journey in this lifetime. Your mother is your source of life, and frequently, she is your source of healing. Are you feeling positive or negative energies towards mother? Are you too close to mother – perhaps her confidante – or do you take care of her emotional needs? Did you feel like you got too much of mother energetically or not enough? Do you feel anger, resentment or hatred toward mother? Are you blaming mother for something in your life? Do you feel that your mother should stop controlling your life? Do you feel like you have a good relationship with mother, yet something is still missing in life?

The narrow perception of the child impacts the adult's whole lifetime if it is not shifted to an adult's big picture perception. The child can never fully understand the relationship between her mother and her father, or the relationship between mother and her parents or grandparents. Energetically, the child can only get to her father through her mother. This dynamic generally pertains to both daughters and sons. As a late teen or adult, it is never too late to shift to an adult's big picture perception.

Give and Take

As mentioned in the last two chapters about Mothers and Daughters, you learned your energetic emotional response patterns in relationship with your mother. As a baby or child, if you felt that mother was emotionally absent, life may not have felt like a safe or welcoming place for you. If you were the baby or child that unconsciously sacrificed or martyred yourself to care for your mother's emotional needs, you learned to GIVE rather than to TAKE from mother. When the child is in a long-term pattern of giving to the parent, rather than taking from the parent, it is energy dead-ening for the child. This emotional pattern goes against the natural order of the family system. The natural order is for the baby or child to TAKE from the mother or to RECEIVE from mother. The reaching out movement of the baby towards mother takes place at birth. The baby seeks to connect with mother, to know that the world is a safe, loving and joyful place to be. If mother is not present energetically or emotionally at birth, the baby's attempts to connect emotionally are blocked, and the baby's body tightens or contracts in response. When the world feels like a scary place to the newborn child, the child naturally takes on an emotional response strategy to ensure survival. Hyper-vigilance, lack of trust or lack of safety may be that emotional response. Rather than easily taking love and nourishment from mother, deeply breathing in life force energy and flowing with life, the child may begin lifelong patterns of rigidity in the body, the need to control and giving to mother rather than taking energetically for survival.

The daughter who attempts to give to mother by carrying or sharing mother's emotional burdens, places herself above mother energetically. "I have to take care of her. She is emotionally needy." Life force energy and the breath of life from mother can't fully enter someone who is feeling bigger than or superior to her mother. The child unconsciously feels, "I will do anything to keep you emotionally well mother because I rely on you for survival." "I will give you everything, even sacrifice myself for your wellbe-ing." A child innately knows that her own wellness is connected to mother's wellness. A client recently stated this simply: "If mother is happy, everyone is happy."

Give and Take as Adults

Family systems marry family systems for a reason. Give and take pat-terns develop in family systems. What childhood give and take patterns did you develop? How are these patterns impacting your life as an adult? Are you able to take or receive, or are you a chronic giver? As much as this might feel like a virtue, it is not. Relationships of give and take develop early in life with your biological mother. For adopted children, if you feel as if mother abandoned you, you may carry the feeling of being abandoned physically, emotionally, psychologically or spiritually in all your relationships at some point. You may struggle to receive and be the chronic giver. Healing comes in developing compassion for your biological mother and your biological father. They did the best they could for you. If you were adopted, your biological parents may not have felt ready to be good parents and so they gave you up for adoption, hoping you would be placed with a good family. Interestingly, both families in adoptions carry trauma around birth. One family often cannot have children, or for some reason decides not to have biological children, and that may have underlying unresolved transgenerational trauma issues, and the other is giving up their children. It's important to realize that your parents did the best they could with the emotional upbringing and support they received from their family system. If you are an adult, it's time to transition from your childhood emotional energy and into your adult emotional energy, into patterns of self-soothing, self-parenting, self-care and self-love.

Give and take becomes a major issue within intimate partnerships. In a healthy relationship, the person needs to give only what the other can comfortably receive energetically. When the give and take is not somewhat balanced in a partner relationship, the one who gives too much may tend to damage or destroy the relationship. This happens when one partner constantly gives more than the other person can emotionally receive. Many givers have trouble receiving. Many people give as a means of unconscious control in a relationship or it may create a feeling of innocence: "I'm doing the best I can in this relationship - they are to blame if things go wrong."

This lack of balance is felt emotionally in the body of both partners. These inner feelings come from their early relationships with their mothers. When we continually take, but we're unable to give back in return, we are not fully able to receive what is given to us. We begin to feel small in the relationship, we fail to thrive, and we feel weak in our role as an intimate partner. It's the energy dynamic we experienced with mother. The individual that feels like the small one – the child - in the relationship loses their self-esteem and self-respect, and they feel the desire to leave in order to regain it. For the constant taker, two dynamics may be present. The taker may not be able to easily receive, and/or the taker may not be able to easily give. Receiving may be difficult if the person feels energetically depressed or sad. Giving might be difficult if the individual unconsciously gave too much energetically to their mother in childhood. The unconscious energy and belief behind the actions of the taker might be, "this feels like the emotional turmoil of my mother. I gave everything I had to my mother and I have nothing left to give to you (the intimate partner)." Not surprisingly, this is a common dynamic for sons and daughters. This is energetically unhealthy in a relationship. Healing comes in giving these burdens that were taken on in childhood back to their rightful owner, which in these situations is mother, although the unresolved emotional trauma may also belong to other members of the family system. When these burdens are successfully passed back with love, without blame or judgement, and with the inner conviction that mother is strong enough to carry her own emotional burdens, the person will begin to shift their relationship dynamics with others as well.

Too much taking that is not balanced with giving may create a sense of being emotionally overwhelmed and there may be the need to push the partner away or put distance between the two of you. The constant receiver may also feel the need to do something to hurt the giver. They may cheat on the partner who gives too much or do something else that ends the relationship. The one with the energy of the child or the constant taker in the partnership feels the need to leave in order to grow up and mature. Often, they don't consciously understand why they are hurting their partner.

Family Balance

How does all this taking and receiving from the parent balance out? It appears to be so out of balance. The grandparent gives to the parent, who then turns around and gives to the child. Older siblings give to younger siblings in descending order of age, not the reverse, unless there is a family dynamic such as someone with a challenge in the family that requires extra care. If you are meddling in the life of an older sibling, it's time to stop, regardless of what they are doing with their life. You will only suffer. Again, if care is given out of duty or obligation, or with resentment and not love, it is energy deadening for the child that helps. As the child shifts into adolescence and then adulthood, they may become a parent and balance the energy of the family system by giving to their children. If the adult doesn't have children they may care for an aging parent later in life or for others in the family system or greater community, and in this way, bring give and take balance into the family system and the greater community system.

When there is an inappropriate energetic giving toward mother, rather than taking or receiving from mother, an unconscious energetic bonding wound may occur between the mother and the child. Both the mother and the child may be weakened by this inappropriate exchange of energy. The child doesn't feel mother's love even if mother is consciously doing a pretty good job. The child feels something is missing. The child may feel energetically abandoned. An emotional attachment wound with mother may set up an energetic merging with mother or a rejection of mother. The child, who is now an adult, needs to acknowledge their unconscious role in setting up this dynamic and take responsibility to shift it.

Feelings of Failure

A child can never be successful at giving to the parent, unless it's in giving gratitude, returning love in a healthy way, or giving when the parent is in old age and requires care. As mentioned above, caring for a parent needs to be done from a place of love rather than through resentment, duty or obligation. It's energy deadening to give to a parent through a sense of obligation or while carrying a feeling of resentment. This is called living in agency. An adult that is expecting a parent to change in some way, expecting an apology from a parent or expecting some other shift to occur, needs to stop waiting. The adult child can only change him or herself. Do you need to shift any relationship in your life to begin giving through love rather than resentment?

The daughter who gives rather than takes from her mother may feel uncomfortable in her body. She may feel uncomfortable when she attempts to stay in her body energetically. The child who gives energetically to a parent or the child that attempts to hold the parents' relationship together may tend to feel like a failure in many life experiences, even if they are successful. Giving, rather than taking from the parent, goes against the energetic flow of the family system and the universe. This sense of failure may create a feeling that you are not successful in other areas of life as well. It may feel like some barrier is holding you back. You may feel like a failure much of the time, even when things are going well. You may feel like you are not enough or somehow inadequate. If this is your situation, it may be time to shift this energetic dynamic in your life, learning to receive as well as give.

We can connect to our mother unconsciously through carrying or sharing her emotional burdens, following her energetically, or taking on her qualities and behaviours. We may even get to atone for her if harm was done to another. This is how we unconsciously show our love and loyalty to mother when we have consciously or unconsciously rejected her or merged with her. As well, if you find yourself attempting to do things in life the opposite to mother, hence emotionally and energetically rejecting her, mother's patterns may show up in your life or in the lives of your children or grandchildren. The family system doesn't tolerate the child rejecting the parent. Rejection of a parent shows ingratitude for receiving the gift of life, regardless of how challenging your childhood was, or your life might be. This attitude has the underlying essence of being a victim of life, rather than being a full participant in choosing the human lifetime you have. The child may struggle until they heal their own emotional wounds and acknowledge the big picture of the family system.

The Mediator

I have discovered that many women are the mediators of the family. This dynamic frequently creates unwellness. Since childhood, the daughter has been energetically standing between mother and father, consciously or unconsciously attempting to hold the relationship or the marriage of her parents together. She attempts to mediate any conflict. She takes care of mother and she takes care of father. These dynamics place the child in a dangerous position energetically. The child may suffer. The child becomes too big energetically in the family system. It is too much for the child to carry. The child stands energetically superior, judging mother and/or father as not enough and weak or flawed in some way. Carrying this energy in their body, the child (who may certainly be an adult) can become unwell in some way.

As well, the child may energetically step into the marriage as either mother or father's energetic or emotional partner. For example, if the child determines that father is not doing a good enough job supporting mother, the child unconscious says, "I will be there for you mother." The child sacrifices her own wellbeing to care for mother's wellbeing. The child tends to side with one parent or the other. The child may reject one parent and merge with the other. Sometimes the child becomes one parent's confidante. This may feel special, but it is not. The child does not see the big picture. All of these situations are energetically deadening for the child. The child is meant to remain outside the marriage or partnership of the parents. The relationship of the parents is not the business of the child. The child is meant to be the small one, not the big one. To discover this can feel like a rude awakening for many people. To discover that you are energetically the small one in the family can also be very liberating emotionally.

Many children with symptoms of unwellness carry this energy dynamic. The physical, emotional, psychological, mental, financial and spiritual burdens of the parents are weighing down the child. When mother and father do their own emotional healing work and take care of their own emotional needs, the child no longer needs to fulfil this role in the family and is free to live his or her own fate. The child is free to let go of these burdens and to simply TAKE from the parents rather than to GIVE to them. This aligns the child with the natural flow of love, and the child often feels this transformation in their body when they show gratitude for life, unless other energetic issues are still unresolved.

Symptoms

Persistent conditions, chronic illness and repetitive life patterns do flow transgenerationally down from great grandmother to grandmother to mother to daughter. Some women fit into their family system by being unwell in some way. Some daughters are sad and depressed, some get cancer, some have their first child die, some carry fear around childbirth and some must remain vigilant or feel that something terrible will happen. Some women identify themselves with their symptoms. They refer to their symptoms as "my cancer" or "my arthritis". They have let the symptoms possess them. If each generation of the women in the family develop a particular condition; it may reveal the tendency in the family to carry the emotional burdens of others, or to live in agency with mother or others. This doesn't always have to show up in the woman's line of the family either. For example, it can show up in other ways such as the men in the family tending to leave the relationship or be energetically absent, the men struggling to commit in relationships or the men being emotionally distant or exhibiting addictive behaviours.

In a systemic constellation, the representative placed for a symptom frequently supports a woman in some way or it may morph into a person in the family system who is attempting to be seen and acknowledged. The symptom may be mother, an institutionalized aunt, a mourning grandmother or a missing child in the family system. Remember that missing children include those miscarried or aborted, those given up to adoption or fostering, those institutionalized and those that die young or tragically. Many symptoms may be serving to entangle you with unresolved ancestral emotional trauma. As the family system seeks balance and seeks to heal, you may be drawn to those who have died and/or those who are simply seeking to be acknowledged or seen by the family system.

A symptom or condition that may have some origins in genetics may also have a strong epigenetic emotional underpinning holding the symptom in place. Emotional events may be impacting the expression of the genes epigenetically, and not shifting the underlying DNA structure genetically. Some emotional or energetic patterns may be travelling down transgenerationally through the family system. Is arthritis, depression, anxiety, vigilance, immune issues, sadness, anger, guilt, resentment, shame or losing a child your unconscious way of remaining connected to your mother? It is important to understand that it is time to build a healthy, balanced relationship with mother and to find new positive ways to remain connected to her. Emotional response patterns may contribute strongly to conditions such as breast cancer. Is breast cancer your unconscious way of remaining connected to your mother or grandmother when your physical relationship is or was problematic? The messages of the body about breast cancer may reveal that you are living in agency with others. Alternatively, you might be carrying heavy negative emotions such as rage, hatred, regret, sorrow or resentment for your mother or grandmother. You may have no conscious idea why you always feel this way. Unfortunately, you may be creating a malignant soup for the cells of your body. Living in agency is energy deadening. Agency is taking care of the needs of others before you care for your own needs. Your own needs seem to come last on your priority list. For those who have died, in this situation an obituary might say that the individual was always thinking about the needs of others and always caring for others. Many in society today mistakenly believe that self-sacrifice and martyring oneself are virtues. In reality, they are a form of self-abandonment or self-betrayal, and this behaviour may make you unwell in some way. Self-sacrifice and martyring are points to be experienced on a spectrum of duality. Wellness comes in shifting out of victimhood and self-sacrifice to care for yourself first, before turning around and giving to others.

If you are living in agency, the message of your body through a symptom may be saying, "take care of yourself first, then you can assist or help others!" A client used the example given by the airlines in their safety talks about what to do if the oxygen masks drop down in front of you in an emergency. You are to put your own oxygen mask on first and then help others. This is the same philosophy. You can only help others in a healthy way if you take care of your own wellbeing first. This is not selfish behaviour. Once you take in your birthright – breathing in your full life force energy that was passed to you through your mother – then you can give to others in a healthy way. If you have symptoms, your body may be waiting for you to stop abandoning yourself. If one symptom after another occurs in your life, your body is simply waiting patiently for you to give it unconditional love. It is time to stop living in agency with others. It is time to learn how to say NO when your body wants you to say NO and to do it without carrying any feelings of guilt. It is time to develop a healthy energy boundary with others to support your own wellbeing. You are fortunate that your body is that patient with you.

Some symptoms may send you to bed for much needed sleep or down time, and other symptoms may set up an energy boundary for you if you don't have a healthy boundary with those around you. The symptom may keep you at home or keep you from participating in unhealthy activities with others. It is time to develop a healthy boundary, reducing your body's need to create a boundary for you through symptoms. We begin to shift our world when we take responsibility for our own wellbeing and seek to understand how we might be consciously or unconsciously contributing to our own symptoms, conditions and lack of wellbeing. In what way do you carry the same symptoms as your mother or other women in your family system?

Gender Bias

Let's look at gender bias in the family system. What happens when there is a gender preference in the family system? Many cultures favour the boy child. Many pregnant women carry a longing for a child of one gender or the other. They may fear having a child of the "wrong" gender. This fear transfers to the baby as a feeling of not being wanted, not being loved or not being good enough. Many women around the world abort children of the "wrong" gender. For example, many pregnant women may feel like a failure, or threatened and unsupported, if the boy child they longed to present to their partner turns out to be a girl child. The opposite may also happen. The child feels this rejection from the time of conception energetically. It makes the world feel like an unsafe place for the surviving child.

In some families, there is a sense that it is not okay to be a girl or it's not safe to be a girl. Perhaps the family feels that girls need to be coddled or protected. These daughters may grow up feeling unsafe in everything they do. They may literally fear life. Other families may openly express that boys don't cry. In some families when dad is away, little boys are expected to be the man of the house. These dynamics may create energetic entanglements for the child. The child may feel like a failure in everything they do. They may impact the child's sense of wellbeing and safety, possibly affect the child's comfort with their gender, or create relationship issues throughout life.

Figure out what gender bias you carry inside. How did your mother and grandmothers speak about or act toward men and women? Did they favour men or did they favour women? Was one gender or the other considered weaker and in need of care by the other? Do you consider men to be the weaker sex – unable to look after themselves without a capable woman around? This may indicate a male gender bias. As a daughter of the household, was the big goal to find a great marital partner for you – someone who would take care of you? You can have a gender bias against men or women. If you are a woman, do you consider yourself to be an exception to the stereotypes you carry about most other women? This will tell you that you have a female gender bias. You carry an unconscious bias against yourself. You will need to address this family gender bias and minimize the impact it has on your life and relationships if you want to learn to love yourself unconditionally and relate well to your intimate partner or to Self. This gender bias may pass down to your children.

Time to Transition

If you are an adult daughter still expecting more from your mother, or you still yearn for your relationship with mother to be different, then it is time for you to take action. It is up to you to shift the unhealthy relationship with mother into a healthy relationship, whether mother is still alive and well on the planet, or whether she has passed to the other side. It is never too late to shift this relationship. You are the one who needs to change your way of being in the world. You need to address your own inner wounds from early childhood. Many of these wounds may be unconscious. It is up to you to make an intentional decision to transform your own life and the world around you. You are not going to change a parent unless they choose to change themselves. Prior to birth, you chose to have this parent behave in this fashion towards you. They are doing what you asked them to do for your own spiritual development and growth.[18] It is time to be grateful for the experiences of your life, regardless of how difficult they have been. You have survived – you have lived through them. Now it is time to thrive. What skills, gifts and talents have you developed in life through your experiences and the relationship you had with your parents? We all have spiritual and development goals. Learn the lesson offered to you through your life challenges and move forward with the knowledge. What have you learned through the experience of depression? What have you learned through the experience of abuse? What have you learned through a marital breakdown? What have you learned through the experience of cancer? What have you learned through the experience of oppression? What emotional talents did you develop by living these particular experiences? Sometimes it's about deciding whether you want to continue feeling right

---

18 There are many sources for this philosophy of life, including: Hasselmann, V. & Schmolke, F. *(1993). Archetypes of the Soul.* Munich, Germany: Wilhelm Goldmann Verlag, München. Hoodwin, S. (1995/2013). *Journey of Your Soul: A channel explores the Michael Teachings (2nd ed.).* Berkeley, California: North Atlantic Books. Stevens, J. & Warwick-Smith, S. (1990). *The Michael handbook: A channeled system for self understanding.* Sonoma, CA: Warwick Press.

and superior as a victim, or whether you want to live with wellbeing. This is a sticking point for many people and the place where many get stuck in life.

Develop Compassion

A significant dynamic of the systemic healing process for a daughter is to develop compassion for the life journey of her mother regardless of what mother may have done or not done. It's in developing an understanding that mother did the best she could with the emotional upbringing she experienced. If you were raised in a home with addictive behaviours or abuses, there are family wounds ancestrally behind your parents or in their current lives still waiting to be acknowledged. If a daughter continues to reject her mother, or to blame or judge her in some way, the daughter tends to struggle in life in some way. Healing comes for you when you learn to take in the full love of mother and father in a healthy way – JUST THE WAY IT WAS OR IS OFFERED TO YOU. You need to stop expecting it to be other than the way it is or was. You transform your world when you stop expecting more from your parents. Each adult must learn to self-parent by the age of eighteen or the age of majority or adulthood in your region of the world. Healing comes for you when you develop compassion for mother and father and their respective life journeys. What did they experience in their childhood? What adversity happened to the earlier generations of grandparents and ancestors? What you reject or judge in mother and father, you reject and judge within yourself. You develop compassion for yourself when you have compassion for mother and father.

Release the Unconscious Burdens

If you are still energetically and emotionally giving to your mother, unable to take from her, you may be carrying her emotional burdens. Systemic healing work and rituals need to be done to pass the burdens back to her. If you want emotional wellbeing this cannot be avoided. You may go through adulthood unaware that you are carrying this emotional burden or the fate that belongs to your mother. If you have back, shoulder or neck issues, you may want to sort out whether you are carrying a heavy emotional burden on your back for your mother, your father or someone else in the family system. That seems like a figure of speech, however, it may be your reality. In some situations, you may have selected a life path or a career that allows you to continue caring for others, the lifelong emotional response pattern you developed with your mother. You may be a doctor, nurse, counsellor, psychologist or member of the clergy to follow the emotional response pattern you learned in childhood. You may select a life path where you seek justice if life didn't or doesn't feel fair. You may select a life path in healing if you feel hurt inside.

Part of your healing process is learning to work with others without being in agency with them. Many seek to heal themselves through helping or healing others. Be forewarned that many healing and helping professionals set up co-dependent relationships with their clients or patients. If you are attempting to fix your client or patient or their life, then you are living in one of these relationships. No one is broken. Individuals need to take responsibility for their own wellbeing if they have the mental capacity to do so – a second party cannot do this for them. If the practitioner is stuck attempting to fix the client, the co-dependent relationship may continue for years with little energetic shift occurring, especially if the practitioner is still quite wounded themselves inside. If you connect with a body focused integrative wellness practitioner, and take responsibility for your own wellbeing, they may be able to guide you through a process to release these emotional burdens from your body. This is one of the best investments you will ever make in your life. You will then be free to live your own fate, assuming you don't have multiple layers of emotional burdens or energetic entanglements to address. With awareness, you can peel back the emotional layers of the onion, one layer at a time, when the greater collective field feels you are ready.

Dates and Anniversaries

Be aware of any significant dates or anniversaries in your family system. I'm not just speaking of formal wedding anniversaries, but also of anything that occurs on the same day as something that occurred earlier, perhaps years apart. An anniversary may be an event that occurs in your life at about the same age of another emotional trauma for your mother, grandmother or other family member. Dates may connect an emotional transgenerational trauma to the onset of physical, emotional, psychological, spiritual, financial, mental or relationship symptoms. Symptoms that reveal an energetic entanglement often occur within about a year of an unresolved emotional event or trauma. Perhaps mother died, and you carry feelings of regret or guilt. "I will remember you mother - merge with you - by not living life fully." Perhaps mother died of cancer and exactly a year later you were diagnosed with another form of cancer or another symptom. "Mother, I regret that I always fought with you, and through this symptom, I will unconsciously show my love and loyalty to you." "Mother, it is through unwellness that I fit into this family." Perhaps mother was in a serious accident at age 25 and then you suddenly find yourself without a job at age 25. These timely events don't tend to be a coincidence. They tend to have systemic healing meaning or significance for you if you pay attention to them.

Living Gratitude

When you are ready to transform your world, you look to your mother, whether she is living or transitioned to the other side and you say, "THANK YOU FOR GIVING ME LIFE!" "I SAY YES TO LIFE AS IT WAS GIVEN TO ME!" You set aside your narrow childhood perception. You shift childhood inner body images. You are not forced to forget anything that happened to you. However, as a daughter of the family system, you take the time to look at the big picture of your family system and the experiences of many of your ancestors to understand your place in it, your mother's place in it and your father's place in it; and acknowledge how each of you was impacted by it.

Family

Patriarchy

Written December 18, 2014

Is your live impacted by patriarchy – perhaps a heavy influence of the church in the past - or even the present? Is there patriarchy showing up in family constellations of your family system? As I have suggested before, if you want more information on family constellations themselves, please go to the extensive suggested reading list at the back of this book. As a family system is mapped out with either live representatives or markers on the floor, or a concern of the client is addressed in the same way, does patriarchy show up in the way a constellation facilitator works with the client. This chapter and several others to follow in this book, and Book 4 of this series, are going to address a few controversial topics of concern to individuals that search online for "Bert Hellinger" or "Family Constellations," and they discover that the man and the work has critics. I am not going to address the critics themselves, but I will address the topics of their criticism. First, I will mention that most individuals who become well-known or famous do tend to have critics. One human being can't be everything to everybody. In the field of psychotherapy, Freud had his critics and Jung had his critics. Hellinger came out of the field of psychotherapy as well. As bright innovative thinkers branch off from the parent ideology of their time with their own theories, those who feel threatened in some way often become critics. This dynamic is similar to the adolescent seeking to separate themselves from their parent and choosing blame and judgement to create the distance they desire. The critics of diverse thinkers, through their fear of the unknown, often seek safety within the status quo.

Family Constellations

Bert Hellinger branched off from the therapies accepted in the late 1980s with his phenomenological approach called Family Constellations. He wasn't the first person to use the phrase Family Constellations to describe therapy approaches for family issues, and Hellinger intentionally never copyrighted his concept of Family Constellations. I'm certain that would have been problematic since Family Constellation was a term used by other practitioners before him. For example, Walter Toman authored his book *Family Constellation: Theory and Practice of a Psychological Game* in 1961.[19] His work was around sibling relationships and dynamics in family systems. Nevertheless, it is generally recognized worldwide that Hellinger is the founder of a particular phenomenological systemic approach called Family Constellations. It is used to address transgenerational family issues and concerns and many other human, organizational and nature systems issues. Hellinger's uniqueness was his concentration on phenomena that went beyond well-known contemporary work with families in the 1980s. At that time, some therapists would drag many family members into therapy sessions, even ones that lived afar, to address issues impacting more than one generation. Hellinger's work was controversial, focusing on phenomenology, experience and the study of consciousness. He developed a series of principles that underlie his work, such as everyone has a right to belong. However, there is no set way to do constellations and the current work of facilitators utilizing his principles runs the whole gamut of diverse practice. This chapter will bring awareness to areas of your own systemic healing journey that may relate to patriarchy and may need to be addressed to attain wellbeing. I will utilize the philosophy and principles from Hellinger's approach, aiding you in peeling back another layer of the onion, the systemic emotional onion.

Bert Hellinger

Bert Hellinger is thought to be the originator of Family Constellations or Systemic Constellations as it is frequently referred to today because of its diverse practise with organizations and nature as well as family systems. When the work of family constellations is taken out of context, or

---

19 With a focus on sibling order in the family, Walter Toman wrote a number of books including: Toman, W. (1961). *Family constellation: Theory and practice of a psychological game.* New York, NY: Springer Pub Co. Toman, W. (1992). *Family constellation: Its effect on personality and social behavior.* New York, NY: Springer Pub Co. (Original work published in 1961 by Verlag C. H. Beck, Munich, Germany)

you attempt to fit it into a different model, confusion, misunderstanding and distrust may arise. I was asked by an acquaintance who had done an Internet search for Family Constellations and Bert Hellinger to address these controversial topics. I thought the challenge would help me integrate the light and the shadow of the topic. I chose not to go back into the many constellations books, or to the DVDs or writing of Hellinger I have in my possession, for my responses. This follows the philosophy that you cannot define a word by using the same word in your definition. Why is Family Constellations so diverse? I sense that Hellinger did not copyright Family Constellations as one package because he did not want to limit the potential and possibilities that Family Constellations held. Interestingly, Hellinger is still alive and practicing today. His concept of Family Constellations continues to evolve and change making it obviously difficult to copyright. Each practitioner comes away from a Family Constellations training with their own perspective around the principles of the work, and it is common for them to add their own background to their constellations facilitation approach with clients. There are one to one client sessions and larger work-shops, which are significantly different. However, the underlying principles used in both are generally the same. You will appreciate the work of some facilitators and reject the work of others - that is inevitable. I will speak from my own experience of family constellations after training with many facilitators from around the globe.

Controversy #1: Patriarchy

Borrowing from The Free Dictionary online,[20] patriarchy is defined as:

- A social system in which the father is the head of the family.

- A family, community or society based on this system or governed by men.

- Dominance of a society by men, or the values that uphold such dominance.

---

20 Patriarchy, The Free Dictionary by Farlex, Retrieved December 18, 2014 from http://www.thefree-dictionary.com/patriarchy

- The collection of men in positions of power, exerting such dominance.

The Questions Asked: Is it true in family constellations that there are dominant overtones of patriarchy? Is the father considered to be the head of the household and is he not to be questioned with regards to the structure of the family dynamic?

My response: I don't believe there are dominant overtones of patriarchy in the principles of family constellations. I have had this discussion with other facilitators and there is no sense of patriarchy in the work. It is sometimes the case that the facilitator is strongly influenced by patriarchy in their own life and this becomes their blind spot in their work. We are never as effective as facilitators if we fail to acknowledge our own blind spots and do our own systemic healing work around them to reduce their impact on our practice with clients. This is relevant for helpers in any walk of life. Like anything, family constellations tend to be interpreted differently by each facilitator, although the many principles underlying the work do tend to have a certain universal ring of truth to them. Thousands of constellations, and the work of many facilitators all over the world, reveal similar dynamics showing up one time after another in different family systems, and these dynamics are accepted as the orders of family in Family Constellations. Are there exceptions to these orders? – All the time. In my way of thinking and in my work, life begins with the father's sperm, and once the ova of the woman is impregnated, mother carries life within her womb. That is why I tend to set up the father first in a family of origin constellation, and then the mother stands to his left. Representatives set up for most family systems just seem to feel energetically more settled or comfortable when standing in this arrangement. Setting up father first does not indicate patriarchy. There are times that this order does not feel right for the family system and it is okay to change it. Family systems with same gender parents will feel into their own order of family.

The Field Aligns the Family

The energy of the greater collective field aligns the family system. Many persons support placing the protector of the family system first – the one who tends to face the outside world the most in the first position. Traditionally, but not always, this was the male, the father of the family system, but this is certainly shifting in many family systems today. This is followed by the nurturer – the one who bears the children and keeps the family home functioning for the raising of children. Regardless of societal shifts over the past few decades, with more women working outside the circle of their home, the woman still bears the children. Traditionally, the mother was the nurturer of the family system. This all sounds very old fashioned and it may instantly trigger a reaction in you if you have worked hard to change this traditional dynamic. You may be especially triggered if you have rejected your own family system or the way you were raised. If you are defensive or emotionally triggered by these statements, it's important to explore your relationship with your own mother and father and address any unresolved emotional wounds you experienced through your family system. You may also need to explore your religious background for patriarchal stances, practices and dogma that underpinned the greater system that influenced your family of origin. Father then mother does not set up a hierarchy, just as the first person to arrive in a circle is not the head of the circle. If you view it as a hierarchy then you need to work out what emotionally underlies that perspective. Father and mother standing together sets up a relationship that supports the family system. The institution of marriage didn't always exist. It was initially embraced to keep the man from leaving a woman who was pregnant, or a woman with children, without protection and support. A woman was more vulnerable to environmental threats when she was pregnant, or she had children in tow. Marriage, or some other union rite of passage, depending on the society, was a matter of survival for the human species. Today the law in many countries enforces this union dynamic with or without marriage. Set family dynamics have never been a given, as they vary greatly around the world or within societies. In some societies, there may be multiple partners in the relationship to maintain the family unit. In some societies, the adage, it takes a village to raise a child is literally a recognized family dynamic in place. In many societies, grandparents may play a very significant role in childrearing, nurturing and passing on transgenerational wisdom to the next generation. In other societies, the value of grandparents and those who are aging is not recognized in this way and they often do not pass on the family wisdom or stories. Within the principles of Family Constellations, there is priority given to those who came first, and in the family of origin that is the father and the mother.

Biological Evolution is Slow

Biologically, and over millennia, in all societies the women have carried the developing baby in their wombs and given birth to the children. That is a common factor in family systems around the world. From that point in time, family systems vary. Traditionally, women were involved in nurturing the children, preparing the food for the children and keeping the home or shelter suitable for the family's diverse needs. A few decades of the women's movement and the work of the feminist movement, and women working in greater numbers in the outside workforce, has not changed that fundamental energy dynamic in ancestral families of origin. There is no prejudice or discrimination present in this discussion. We look back to see what is or was. We look at the big picture of roles in family systems, communities and societies. Each family system is unique and contextual. We look at whether an individual was born into a patriarchal or matriarchal system, or neither. We look to see if gender bias exists in the family system. We feel into the energetic dynamic within each family system. Recognizing an individual's emotional woundedness, we sort out whether a person grew up in a family system impacted greatly by patriarchic mindsets. This is an important aspect of systemic healing work that needs to be embraced.

After thousands of constellations, it was evident to Hellinger that the family of origin was healthier when it was set up as follows: begin with the father and move to his left with the mother, to her left the oldest child, then the second oldest child, down to the youngest child on the far left. The generations of ancestors stand behind the father and mother in support. Energetic entanglements throw off this alignment in family systems. All children of the family system need to be accounted for in the family line up or family order, including aborted children, children placed for adoption, miscarried children, stillborn children, missing children, unacknowledged children and children that died young. Each family member belongs and has a place, regardless of what they may have done or not done. The greater collective field doesn't tolerate a family member being excluded. The family system struggles with imbalance until each member is welcomed. In some family systems, it may phenomenologically feel right to place mother first and then father. Sometimes father is missing. It may seem that mother has a greater protective, supporting role in the family system. Perhaps mother is the one facing the outer world most of the time. Being absent is not a reason to energetically shift the order of family. Each person has a right to belong. For example, the biological parents of an adopted child are very much present energetically in the life of the child, even though they are often absent physically. Interesting challenges occur if an adopted child meets their biological parents. It is the biological father, then the biological mother and then the child(ren) from oldest to youngest who are placed from right to left in the family of origin when adoption has occurred. The adoptive parents can also be placed in the constellation in gratitude for their contribution to the child's life. As mentioned before, the field does not tolerate exclusion. That is another Hellinger principle extending from the concept that everyone has a right to belong. There are other examples of the father being incapacitated in some way. In this family, there may be a shift in the family order depending on who tends to face the outer world more strongly for the family system. It may or may not mean a shift in the order of family, however, it should not be assumed.

Does it feel patriarchal to you to have father in the furthest right position? It might, especially if you feel wounded by patriarchy in a significant way. Nevertheless, it is not meant to be patriarchal. The greater collective field does not dwell on gender/sex as dualities, but rather as aspects of one spectrum. The greater field is different than human beings who construct duality to experience separation and division. Individuals who embrace a patriarchal system, or those who haven't healed from wounds being raised in one, may feel or misinterpret this systemic constellation family arrangement as patriarchal. Looking at the big picture, in the spiritual realm there is no gender. For our journey to planet Earth as human beings, before birth we decide our gender and also decide whether a greater male energy (more goal oriented) or female energy (less goal oriented) will help us reach our spiritual development and growth for this lifetime. You can be a man with higher female energy or a woman with higher male energy. There is a whole spectrum of diversity. If you go inward, you will know if you carry more male or female energy for this lifetime.

Same Gender Partnerships

Family constellations are not all about heterosexual partnerships. I am not excluding same gender/sex couples in this description. In same gender partnerships, the individuals will energetically know their place on the right or left of one another. This has nothing to do with social and cultural advancement. Same gender/sex relationships have existed since the beginning of human development. This right or left positioning in the family of origin shows what is energetically revealed when a constellation is set up for a family system – when we get out of our rational mind and step back to let the field do its work.

Family Authority and Power Struggles

To address the second part of the question, I have never heard it mentioned in any of my systemic constellation trainings that the authority of the father is not to be questioned. I believe this is a misinterpretation of the work or that something has been said and pulled out of context. Everyone in the family system is held responsible for their own actions, whether these actions occur consciously or unconsciously. Looking to the big picture, respecting the role of mother and father as the givers of life is vitally important. This is a principle within the Family Constellations work of Hellinger. Being able to take in the love of mother and father just as they offer it is essential to wellbeing. Having compassion for the emotional journeys of mother and father is an outcome of looking back to understand the big picture. Those dynamics don't touch on authority. The mature adult and the baby both have equal value in the family system. However, the adult comes first in the family of origin lineup. It is their role to give to the child because they (the adult) have already received more from those behind them (their parents and grandparents). Hence, the adult has energetic priority in relationship to the child(ren) in the family of origin. Taken out of context this statement would be problematic.

Also, the couple relationship takes energetic priority over the parent child relationship because without the couple the child would not exist. That doesn't negate the importance of the parent child relationship. When mothers or fathers put the child first, what is referred to as child-centrism, the child will tend to struggle in life energetically. The mother and father will also tend to struggle as a couple. Sometimes the greater field sets up a dynamic where attention draws heavily to the child. For example, when a child is born with symptoms, conditions, special needs, different needs or a particularly heavy fate in life, one parent may be drawn more heavily to provide support for the child. The other parent may be challenged to find their place in the family situation depending on the emotional resources they gathered through their own family system as a child and how emotionally wounded they are inside. In these situations, the couple relationship will often be a struggle, and frequently it will end. Another difficult parent child relationship that may undermine the priority of the couple relationship is when a child is used as the confidante by one parent and experiences the denigration of the other parent. This is very common with couple separation and divorce. In this situation, the child may energetically suffer. They are manipulated by one parent to believe they (the child) are superior to their other parent. In this situation, the child may even become sick or take on certain behaviours out of unconscious love and loyalty to their maligned parent. The child is being forced to be too big energetically. The child unconsciously uses sickness or unwellness to bring their parents back together, allowing the child to openly love both parents without issue. Energetically, the child has no place in the relationship of their parents. Manipulating a child to take revenge on a former partner has a devastating impact on a family system and the child. When looking back at a family system to understand family authority and power structures, context is everything. Context is vital to understanding family systems and often a systemic constellation reveals an aspect of the family context that is not consciously recognized by the family member involved.

Right to Belong

Looking at some of the key principles of family and systemic constellations helps to alleviate this fear of patriarchy. Everyone has a right to belong in the family system regardless of what they may have done or not done. We shift ourselves from the narrow perception of childhood to the big picture of the whole family system. This does not excuse inappropriate behaviour of any individual. As you know, we cannot change what has occurred in the past. You cannot change others; you can only change yourself. If you experienced behaviour from your mother and father that you judge as inappropriate or unacceptable, then you need to do your own emotional healing work. If you continue to blame and judge those who came before you, you are the one who will suffer or struggle in life. One of the principles is that each person does the best they can with the emotional resources they received through their parents and family system. Your mother did the best that she could do, and your father did the best that he could do. You have done the best you could do to this point in your life. You need to find your way to being grateful for life itself, and to address the rest of your issues within the big picture of your family system.

To expect anything different from your parents other than what was offered to you creates an energetic roadblock in your life. It blocks the flow of love in the family system. To be an adult still expecting something from your parents creates life difficulties. You may struggle if you dispute the principles that "everyone has a right to belong" and "everyone did the best they could," and it may hold you stuck in blame and judgement. You are encouraged to step out of your narrow childhood perception to look back at the bigger family picture. What backgrounds, emotional response patterns and unresolved trauma situations were passed from your great grandparents to your grandparents and from your grandparents to your parents? If you need to, go back another generation or two to find the source of the emotional woundedness in your family system that creates a struggle with patriarchy. Did the woundedness flow through a religious or government institution that upheld patriarchy? You may even want to look at your relationship with your own father.

Family Dynamics in Constellations

During systemic constellations, the facilitator may ask representatives of a family system to shift to different positions. As I mentioned before, the field often seems most comfortable with the father set up on the right, the mother next on his left, etc. It's a family order that many individuals energetically and emotionally yearn for but don't feel within their family system. If the family of origin is set up in a line, many individuals initially feel quite uncomfortable in their own placement within their nuclear family system. Many people are energetically shocked to find themselves set up way over to the left as a younger child in the family system, even though consciously they know that is their right placement. Too often, they have spent their entire life sacrificing themselves in an attempt to carry the emotional burdens of their mother or father, or they have identified with another family member with unresolved emotional trauma, and they tend to feel themselves bigger than the parent or grandparent. The child begins to feel calm as they allow themselves to be the small one in the proper family order. They feel energetically soothed when they allow themselves to take from those who came before them, rather than their old emotional pattern of living in agency - giving, giving, giving – often thanklessly, without caring for their own needs first.

Facilitator Background

The Family Constellation critics specifically point their finger at Bert Hellinger, so let's look briefly at his background. I spent only five days at one of Hellinger's international training sessions in 2012, so I am certainly not an expert on the man himself. Having read many of his books I do feel like I have a strong sense of the man. Regardless, I do recognize with respect his place in Family Constellations work as the founder. As I have mentioned before, honouring lineage is important to energetic wellbeing. Hellinger's work carries the imprint of many others before him, however, it all consolidated for him in a way that was different from all the others. As mentioned before, Hellinger is still alive and going strong in his nineties. He is a very bright, creative and spiritual man. Do I expect him to be other than he is? No, that would require judgement of one that came before me. Has he made mistakes? I am certain that he has. Has he altered his thinking and approach over the years? I believe his life and work has shifted a great deal over the past three decades. Has he been influenced by the input of others and events in his life? Yes, that is certainly the case, as it is for all of us. That is how he first began to understand the greater systemic dynamics of family, by learning from the family systems of other cultures. I believe we have just determined that Hellinger is human, and as with all human beings, we tend to excel when we learn from our missteps. What others might call failure or mistakes are actually wonderful opportunities for learning.

Hellinger's Background

Hellinger evolved as a young adult out of the dynamics of Nazi Germany. He was a youth when the Hitler Youth were being assembled and he refused to participate. Hellinger grew up in a family that resisted nationalism. When he was of age for enlistment, he was recruited to fight in World War II under the ultimate command of Adolph Hitler. When the war ended, he was a prisoner of war in Belgium. Back in Germany after the war, he faced the post-World War II massive system of collective national retribution imposed on Germany by the world. There was extreme repression of nationalistic emotion and energy. Germany was under the microscope of the rest of the world. His nation was viewed as the perpetrator with many victims. After the war, Hellinger became a Roman Catholic priest and spent sixteen years living amongst the Zulu in South Africa. He thought he was going to Africa to change the lives of the people, and to convert them religiously, however, he soon discovered through observation and participation in their culture and daily life that he had a lot to learn from the Zulu and their respectful transgenerational family interaction and dynamics.[21]

Whereas, during the lead up to World War II, and during the war, many members of the Hitler Youth were denouncing their own parents out of loyalty to Hitler and the Nazi movement, Hellinger experienced Zulu youth showing great respect to their parents and ancestors. There was no division between the living and the dead. Hellinger listened, learned and embraced. After sixteen years, he returned to Germany, left the priesthood and began to study various psychotherapy approaches. About seventeen years later, while working along with other colleagues, he developed the phenomenological Family Constellation approach to wellbeing. It was controversial, and some of his early actions were certainly questioned by others. As mentioned earlier, Hellinger has critics. Despite the controversy, the approach continued to develop and evolve. Each new facilitator trained takes the work and makes it their own, drawing from their own background, work, study and life experience. Each facilitator is influenced by their own family system and their ancestors. Each facilitator is impacted

---

21 Hellinger, B., Weber, G., & Beaumont, H. (1998). Love's hidden symmetry: *What makes love work in relationships.* Phoenix, AR: Zeig, Tucker & Co., pp. 327-330.

by their own degree of inner woundedness. One commonality amongst all of my constellation mentors over the years is that they held respect for the ones who came before them - especially the work of Bert Hellinger as the originator of the concept and the phenomenological approach. This is a principle that shows up within Family Constellation practice. This does not mean they agreed with everything Hellinger did or said. Respect does not imply full agreement. Respect implies an agreement to honour the other person as a valuable human being, regardless of their belief system or what they have done.

Hellinger's Influences

How was Hellinger influenced by patriarchy? As mentioned, each facilitator will work from or through their emotional response patterns – their inner emotional woundedness. It is hoped that through training in Family Constellations facilitation that a person will have done some of their systemic emotional healing work and that they came away from the experience understanding the importance of continuing to do so. That they will have made inroads in their systemic healing with mother and father. It is a lifelong journey. Patriarchy underpins many traditional institutions. Within the greater system of Nazism, Hitler had his own sense of the world and who was superior and inferior. He set himself up as an all-powerful father figure. Germany was called a Fatherland rather than a Motherland. As a soldier in the army, Hellinger was within a military system that was historically patriarchal. As a Roman Catholic priest, Hellinger came out of a patriarchal background and belief system. I'm certain that tribal groups in Africa have a certain sense of order to the family system and community. His time amongst them would have influenced Hellinger's way of being in the world. The world of psychotherapy had a major influence in the life of Hellinger. Each of these systems impacted the life, thinking, beliefs and behaviours of Hellinger. I don't know Hellinger's family system history with his own mother and father, or what transgenerational trauma travelled down his family system, but there definitely would have been some.

Just considering the other greater systems surrounding Hellinger, looking at the big picture, helped account for any wayward opinions and mindsets he may have had over the years with a patriarchal bent to them that would have offended the sensibilities of others. Did he soften his stance on many issues as the years went on? – Yes, he did. His approach today is to frequently step back entirely out of influencing the constellation, other than to have his energy present to connect with the energy of the client and their family system. He may not even ask the client for any information before setting up a constellation. He may just set up representatives for the client and others to see what is revealed. Perhaps this is his way of addressing any blind spots he may still carry within himself related to patriarchy or other controversial attributes, if they exist.

Client Constellations

The client usually comes in the door carrying unhealthy inner images about their relationships with mother, father and Self. That dynamic is frequently what keeps them stuck in life or unable to move forward in a healthy way. These feelings and body sensations are what they took out of childhood at the cellular level of memory. Unless we do our emotional healing work, we come out of childhood with a very narrow perspective of life. We see ourselves as the centre of the universe, knowing very little about all those around us, within our family system and beyond. We know little to nothing about the early lives of our parents and grandparents. We remember the dozen or so worst things our mother and father did over the years and we build our story around those details. We have no focus on all that they did that was good or functional, or that ensured our survival out of childhood, even if that meant giving us over to others for caregiving and nurturing. It is important that there is no specific agenda for family constellation work with clients. In fact, less intentional agenda is desirable. Nevertheless, encouraging the client to connect with their ancestral family field is exceedingly valuable. Acceptance of what was and is holds significant value. Guiding clients to develop compassion for the journey of their parents and grandparents needs to be a priority. Since we are fifty percent mother and fifty percent father, what we reject in them we also reject in ourselves. This rejection makes self-love impossible. When we reject aspects of ourselves, remaining in judgement, connecting with our deep authentic inner Self is problematic. One aspect of connecting with our deep inner world is understanding the relationship we have with patriarchy, and the relationship our family system has with patriarchy, particularly as it pertains to identity developing systems such as religious practice, culture or nationalism.

Family

JANUARY

Incest

Written January 27, 2015

In the last chapter I discussed Patriarchy, one of the controversies that swirls around Bert Hellinger and Family Constellations on the Internet. In this chapter I will explore a second controversy.

Controversy #2: Incest

Let's look at the societal definition of incest in the Merriam-Webster online dictionary: "Incest: sexual intercourse between persons so closely related that they are forbidden by law to marry; also: the statutory crime of such a relationship."[22]

An acquaintance asked me the following question: Is it true that Hellinger assigns guilt to the women involved in family situations of incest, that any incest (rape) that occurs between a father and his female daughter is due to the fault of the mother or the spouse who refuses him intimacy? **The acquaintance continued:** This is such a characteristic of what is termed today as *rape culture*, meaning that regardless of circumstance the woman is still held responsible for such a horrific act.

My Response: We do not excuse anyone's inappropriate behaviour. Each person is held responsible for their actions and their wellbeing comes in taking responsibility for those actions. Incest results from energetic entanglement in the family system and lack of healthy boundaries. Rape culture and sexual assault is such a huge topic today, occurring in many institutional settings, both in the past and in the present, that I thought I would systemically address the issue of incest in the family system. It is one of those shadow topics, often taboo or silenced in the family system and also by society. In this chapter, I will first address the topic of incest within a systemic context, including the impact it has on boys, girls, women and men. Second, I will discuss what is meant by genealogical incest.

---

22 Incest. Merriam-Webster Dictionary. Retrieved January 27, 2015 from http://www.merriam-webster.com/dictionary/incest.

Bert Hellinger, considered to be the founder of Family Constellations, has been criticized for his systemic viewpoints on incest. I realize that many critics have taken his comments out of context. Society makes its moral judgements on topics such as incest, taking an individualistic viewpoint. Controversy arises when situations are taken out of context or when individuals expect greater family and systemic dynamics, and greater moral systems, to function in the same way as individualistic societal norms. Systemic constellations look systemically, energetically and contextually at each issue presented, and the outcome tends to reveal insight for the whole family system and the community, not just for the individual. The systemic viewpoint has the potential to bring healing to the whole system. The greater system takes priority over the individual. In the work of systemic and family constellations, the facilitator works with the client and their concern, hopefully looking back at the family system without blame or judgement. If the facilitator, or any counsellor, is unable to look back without assigning blame and judgement, such as in situations where the facilitator experienced sexual assault or abuse at some time in their life, they may have their own blindspots to address before they can be effective for their client or patient. We cannot change the past, so we look back to understand "what was" in the family system that contributed to transgenerational emotional trauma and inappropriate sexual behaviours. We look back to expand our perspective, and to develop compassion for Self and others. Hellinger's book, *Acknowledging WHAT IS: Conversations with Bert Hellinger,* written with Gabriele ten Hövel, addressed many controversial topics. When asked if Hellinger believed in assigning guilt to the women involved in family situations of incest, a comment raised by many of his critics, Hellinger responded,

> I'm not interested in assigning guilt to the women, nor am I interested in assigning guilt to the men, in the sense of judging them. I am interested in uncovering the hidden dynamics and seeking a way to help all the involved parties to find a resolution to the entanglements.[23]

23 Hellinger, B., & ten Hövel, G. (1999). *Acknowledging what is: Conversations with Bert Hellinger* (Trans. C. Beaumont). Phoenix, Arizona: Zeig, Tucker & Co., Inc., p. 116.

He gives an example of a common dynamic in a family system where incest occurs:

> [...], in such a family the woman has pulled away from her partner – not because she's a bad wife, but because she's feeling a pull out of the family. Perhaps she's following a dead sibling, for instance. At the same time, she feels guilty about pulling away and needs a replacement so that she can leave more easily. Then the daughter takes her place. It's not that the mother pushes her to do that, because it's a secret dynamic, a secret agreement. It happens unconsciously, for the mother as well as the daughter, which is why it's so difficult to comprehend. The man carries the foremost guilt because he knows what he's doing, even if he doesn't see the systemic background or understand the dynamics. The woman usually doesn't know what she's doing because her role is unconscious.[24]

Franz Ruppert, in his book, *Trauma, Bonding & Family Constellations: Understanding and Healing Injuries of the Soul*, reveals some of the dynamics in the family system behind a woman who consciously or unconsciously tolerates abuse of her children:

- She has suffered a bonding trauma with her own mother,

- She may have suffered sexual abuse herself and psychologically compartmentalized the abuse, numbing herself to the child's feelings,

- There may be other women in her family system who suffered sexual abuse,

- Her mother passed on to her unresolved emotional trauma and emotional numbing,

- Her own early sexual abuse would create a tendency to reject sexuality, and/or,

---

24 Ibid., p. 117.

- She fears the consequences of speaking up for the child, as it might lead to the end of her security – her marriage – or create shame if the partner goes to prison.[25]

Hellinger says the mother would not be held guilty. He adds,

> They're all entangled. The basic rule still applies, however, that whatever a person does, no matter how entangled he or she is, that person must carry the consequences of the actions. I wouldn't relieve the father of the burden of guilt just because of the entanglements.[26]

Hellinger's motivation in the work is "to help individual people to find a way out of their entanglements, nothing more."[27] He said, "I stay in my own arena."[28] This encourages other facilitators and counsellors to leave their own agendas and outcomes for the work out of the constellation. The client guides the work and the outcome, depending on how much they are able to take in energetically, and the facilitator attunes to their energy and accompanies them on the journey. It is up to the client to acknowledge their need to heal and take responsibility for their own wellbeing.

Long-Term Effects of Incest

People have different levels of emotional resilience and some victims of sexual assault or incest suffer in life to a much greater extent than others. Some numb themselves emotionally to the past, unable to feel anything in life emotionally. Some emotionally compartmentalize the adverse experience. I believe that the greater the amount of unresolved transgenerational ancestral emotional trauma there is in the family system, spread across many family members and generations, the more susceptible a person is to adverse responses to emotional trauma in their current life. The emotional effects may include shame, anxiety, depression, guilt, humiliation, anger, lack of boundaries, inappropriate ideas about sexuality, substance

25 Ruppert, F. (2008). *Trauma, bonding & family constellations: Understand and healing injuries of the soul.* Frome, Somerset, UK: Green Balloon Publishing, p. 165.
26 Hellinger, B., & ten Hövel, G. (1999). *Acknowledging what is: Conversations with Bert Hellinger* (Trans. C. Beaumont). Phoenix, Arizona: Zeig, Tucker & Co., Inc., p. 117.
27 Ibid., p. 117.
28 Ibid., p. 117.

abuse, fears, hyper-vigilance, intimacy problems, inappropriate sexual and other behaviours, nightmares and flashbacks, sleep issues, school issues, mistrust, suicidal thoughts, relationship difficulties, aggressive behaviours, and feelings of self-doubt and isolation. The emotional trauma may contribute to difficulties in adult relationships with partners, instability in the workplace, physical and psychological symptoms, and social behavioural problems, such as criminal actions and transgenerational incest. By taking action, the trauma of sexual assault may not be totally eliminated from your cellular memory, however, the impact it has on your life can be shifted. By taking responsibility for your own life and wellbeing, you can remove yourself from the entanglement that is currently and overwhelmingly driving your life.

Understanding the Greater Family System

Incest is addressed like any other situation within the approach of systemic and family constellations, in that, context is key. Each field of energy or constellation brings forward insight for that particular family system. When the work is taken out of context it tends to become controversial and misunderstood. Often, it is only the client that fully understands or feels what is revealed in a constellation, and sometimes that understanding comes weeks, months or even years later. For this reason, generalizing systemic constellations can be problematic. There are instances when commonalities between constellations can be gathered to help with understanding. Gathering commonalities is a useful process for understanding energetic trends that arise over and over in different family systems. The human mind seeks to find patterns within the chaos of life to make meaning of the world. The orders of family were developed by Hellinger as a result of witnessing similar dynamics occurring continually in different family systems in many regions of the world. For example, there is priority placed on certain family members over others, not in a hierarchical sense, but rather an energetic sense.

How can we benefit from systemic constellations? In systemic constellation work, we are pushed to shift our perspective to the big picture. We are required to step out of our narrow perception of childhood. In childhood, everything is taken personally. We are the centre of our universe. We rarely have an understanding of the big picture. We find ourselves in adulthood knowing little about our parents and grandparents, let alone the details of their emotional past. The young child rarely understands the big picture dynamic between the mother and the father. When addressing incest in a family system, we look back without blame and judgement. Does that excuse the behaviour of the perpetrator? No! Taking the stance of stepping out of blame and judgement, allows space for an emotional shift to begin for the victim, and for the perpetrator. To heal, you need to look at all the energetic dynamics in the family system without turning a blind eye to uncomfortable details. If you have been the victim of incest, you need to discover your energetic role in your family system and understand how you belong or fit into your family of origin and your greater family system.

Incest is an energy dynamic in the family system that is greater than the individual family members involved. We look at what created the emotional behaviour of the mother and the father; or the uncle, the aunt or the grandfather. What unresolved ancestral emotional traumas occurred in the family systems? For example, in the situation of residential schools in Canada, children sexually abused in the schools sometimes became sexual abusers in their own family system later in life. Was incest, sexual abuse or violence a family pattern? Was emotional numbing, splitting off or distancing a family pattern? What happened in this family system to create the dynamics of abuse? There may be many energy dynamics contributing to incest. Like addictions, abuse or incest don't tend to happen without an energetic or emotional transgenerational trauma in the family system behind it. What dynamics created a perpetrator who felt the behaviour of incest was tolerable? The fact that most perpetrators of incest tend to silence their victims in some way, reveals that they know that their behaviour isn't tolerable by the family or society. What we are searching for in this situation is what energy dynamic is pushing them to be perpetrators anyway?

Out of Love and Loyalty

In her book, *Family Constellations: A Practical Guide to Uncovering the Origins of Family Conflict*, Joy Manné expresses the vastness of the love and loyalty of children:

> The love of children for their parents is limitless to the extent of being "crazy." The first time I heard this expression I was indignant, but the more I work as a facilitator, the more I see its truth. Children will do anything for their parents. They are loyal to the point of death. They sacrifice themselves to atone for the guilt of their ancestors so that their family system can find balance again. They become problematic to keep their parents together. They become ill and die in place of their parents. They make themselves available to a parent as a sexual partner. This idea is so upsetting and controversial that I remind you immediately that we are in the field of the systemic conscience, and not in normal ego consciousness: this does not happen, or only very rarely happens, on a conscious level.[29]

Incest in the Family System

As with any dynamic within a family system, those family members involved in incest need to take responsibility for their own actions and for their own wellbeing. If you are the victim of incest, you have a choice to make. You can choose to remain a victim forever and not heal, or you can choose to take responsibility for your own wellbeing and sort things out systemically, energetically and emotionally within your family system, or your community, if that is more appropriate to your situation. It is a choice. Engaging in systemic healing can be a very difficult process for many people. It may open a person to layer upon layer of emotional

---

29 Manné, J. (2009). *Family Constellations: A Practical Guide to Uncovering the Origins of Family Conflict*. Berkeley, CA: North Atlantic Books, p. 35.

trauma that has been silenced by the family system, sometimes for many generations. This can be a very difficult energetic and emotional step. It may take a long time, many years, to feel ready to step up and take action. It will take courage for certain. There may be many energetic dynamics holding a person stuck: blame – someone has to pay, self-blame and shame, I refuse to forget, I'm unworthy – I'm spoiled goods, unconscious love and loyalty – I won't let them hurt my parent or other family member, they won't understand, or I don't trust them. I don't want to lose my mother or father. I don't want to break up my parent's marriage. These old childhood emotional response patterns can be shifted. Healing from incest comes in acknowledging what was and is in the family system. Remember that incest may entangle any number of extended family members as well, including siblings who experienced incest too. A systemic constellation may be helpful in revealing what is suppressed or not consciously acknowledged. A decision to hold in emotional trauma only leads to continued un-wellness. While the past cannot be changed, you can learn a great deal about your family system from it, helping you to shift the inner image you carry about your family system, allowing you to shift your present life, and also to influence your future one baby step at a time. If you were the victim of incest, abuse, sexual assault, rape or any other form of violence, I encourage you to find the courage to take action, to shift and transform your world.

Blame Creates Struggle

Individuals struggle to move forward if they remain stuck in blame. The most difficult part is taking responsibility for your own complicity or entanglement in a family dynamic, whether it is conscious or unconscious. Blame tends to limit the potential for healing. In Book 1 of this Series, *Connect With Your Ancestors*, I wrote several chapters on radical inclusion and the right to belong that are a worthwhile read to understand this powerful energetic dynamic. Also, be aware, if you are seeking to find emotional resolution in the legal world for abuses, incest, or rape, it usually isn't found energetically or emotionally, even if the perpetrator is tried and sentenced for the crimes against you. That is an individualistic viewpoint. The most you can find is space for your own healing to begin. There is a greater field of energy at play that wants to find balance. When the issues of the victim are central to any process or solution, in effect, ignoring the emotional trauma in the family system of the perpetrator, the greater field does not tend to find balance. Many perpetrators were victims first. That doesn't excuse their behaviour, however, it does systemically account for it. We all carry within us the energy of the victim and the perpetrator, sometimes it is from this lifetime and sometimes it extends back through our ancestral family system. Healing is found when the whole big picture is addressed and the emotional needs of everyone are considered to find resolution. Restorative justice has moved in this direction to address victim and perpetrator situations and to begin systemic healing for all individuals involved, their families and their communities.

What About the Perpetrator

When a constellation is set up and it reveals possible incest or rape, the victim tends to remain stuck unless the perpetrator is acknowledged as having a right to belong. Everyone has a right to belong in the family system regardless of what they may have done or not done. When the perpetrator is your father or another beloved family member such as an uncle or grandfather, or someone else you are close to, a huge trust is breached. It is important to acknowledge that sexual abuse and assaults frequently occur against boys and men as well as girls and women. Sometimes we fall into the mindset that girls and women tend to be the victims and men are the perpetrators. This isn't an accurate perception. Stereotypes such as these help to mask many situations of incest, sexual abuse or rape. With incest, there is usually a deep breach of trust. The child, who may be an adult today, developed emotional response patterns to deal with this breach of trust, and to survive this emotional trauma at all costs. The child may have buried all conscious awareness of the abuse, incest or rape – becoming numb emotionally, or splitting off the emotional trauma into a different compartment of their inner world, to enable them to carry on with life. As difficult as it may seem, energetic space has to be given to the perpetrator for overall systemic healing to occur.

Constellations reveal that the journey of both the victim and the perpetrator is relevant to the healing of the greater human system. In effect, victims and perpetrators become members of one another's family systems if that hasn't been recognized already. They become entangled energetically. The perpetrator becomes energetically like a member of your family system. Systemically, we all belong to one big family of energy universally. So it is important how you deal with this person who has perpetrated incest, sexual abuse or sexual assault against you, without rejecting them as a family member. Rejecting a family member creates un-wellness for you, even if you are the victim. The only way to heal is to look back systemically at what was and is. This requires you to look back at *unconscious* actions you may have taken even as a baby or young child. Out of *unconscious* love and loyalty to your family system, as Joy Manné mentioned, the child does what is necessary to survive at all costs. It can really hurt emotionally to find out you were somehow unconsciously involved in the abuse perpetrated against you – without any conscious awareness. Unconscious involvement does not mean that you were responsible for the abuse, incest or rape. You are not guilty of anything – you are definitely not to blame for anything. Although, you do energetically have to take responsibility for unconscious systemic involvement.

Long-Term Effects

The long-term impact of childhood sexual assault varies for each person. With sexual assault in childhood, the perpetrator is frequently someone in a position of trust in the life of the child. This breach of trust is greatly traumatizing. It may be a family member (incest), a teacher, a member of the clergy, a family friend, a coach or a mentor in a position of trust. Using manipulative behaviour, the perpetrator convinces the child or adolescent that the behaviour is okay, that it is a loving gesture, and that it will advance their life in some way. The perpetrator convinces the victim not to report it because they won't be believed or that some adverse situation will occur in their life. If it is incest, the child often fears the break-up of the family if they report the sexual abuse. For situations outside the family, a person often feels they will have to relive the trauma if they report it to the authorities. They often feel that they will not be believed. Many trials have proven these beliefs to be true. Silence often accompanies the occurrence of sexual assault. Silence and lack of emotional processing holds the pain and trauma in the cellular memory of the body. Franz Ruppert explains:

> The earlier in its life a child experiences sexual abuse, the more inten-
> sive the sexual contact, the more extreme the violence, the nearer/
> closer the relative and the more intense the attachment between per-
> petrator and child, the more concealed and serious are the conse-
> quences for the child. There is scarcely any event that harms girls and
> boys more than sexual abuse and sexual violence.[30]

In discussing the confusion and inner conflict faced by the child who is the victim of incest, Ruppert mentioned that the child struggles to:

> Locate where she belongs in the family, she doesn't know whether
> she is a child or an adult. She doesn't know what to do and what not
> to do, what is right or wrong. She can no longer tell the difference
> between truth and lies and thus can no longer distinguish between
> what is illusion and imagination and what is reality.[31]

Looking at Incest Systemically

Within systemic constellations, whether the individual is a male or female victim of childhood incest, they are not rationally or consciously held responsible for their involvement. However, to find systemic healing, they need to take responsibility for their unconscious role in the incest and take responsibility for their own wellbeing. There is a big difference between the two, well beyond semantics. The individual has to take responsibility

---

30 Ruppert, F. (2008). *Trauma, bonding & family constellations: Understand and healing injuries of the soul.* Frome, Somerset, UK: Green Balloon Publishing, p. 159.
31 Ibid., p. 160.

for their role in any event within the family system, whether it was conscious or unconscious, physical, psychological, emotional, spiritual, financial, mental or relational, both as a child and as an adult. Does that mean the child is blamed for abuses or violence against them? No, that is not the case. Utilizing a systemic constellation approach, we look back without blame or judgement towards everyone. There is no fault finding. This is very different than many forms of counselling or psychology or the justice system. We look at the energetic relationships as they were or are in the family system and the greater energy field. That does not mean that we excuse inappropriate behaviours of anyone. We look back to gain an understanding of what was in the family system that contributed to the incidence of incest, sexual assault or abuse. These incidents don't tend to appear out of nowhere. We want to know what the victim is entangled with in their greater family system and what the perpetrator is entangled with in their greater family system. Sexual assault or the energetic dynamics that create it can definitely be transmitted down the generations of family systems transgenerationally. We do encourage you to look back to understand any unconscious actions you may have taken in this lifetime, even in the womb for survival, or to understand the actions and experiences of your parents, grandparents or great grandparents. Acknowledgement that actions may have been unconsciously taken out of love and loyalty to the greater family system, at any stage of gestational or childhood development, is one of the first steps in moving forward.

If involved in systemic constellation work, it is hoped that no harm is done, although many constellations do create great emotional discomfort. This is a step toward greater spiritual and emotional development and growth. The constellation setting hopefully provides a safe place for this systemic emotional healing work to occur. The facilitator continually checks with the client to understand how much emotional healing work a client can tolerate on that day and at that moment of their life. The healing work may create energetic, spiritual, and/or emotional discomfort and growing pains; however, doing harm should be avoided. A person seeking systemic healing needs to be told that they can stop the work if they begin to feel uncomfortable beyond what they are able to feel or address in the moment. This healing work needs to be done in layers, when a person is ready for the next step. The work is done to shift the old energy patterns of the family system, and to shift the emotional response patterns held in the body that developed for survival at a young age. This work is done to address what has been suppressed. The whole process is meant to place the client outside their comfort zone to shift the status quo, and to transform the inner image held in the body around any situation, event or person. The work I do with clients is to get people into their bodies, to increase their capacity to feel, even if it is uncomfortable. There is a saying that we cannot heal what we cannot feel, and with a body focused approach to well-being there certainly seems to be some truth to that phrase. When a family system experiences incest, family members do not have healthy boundaries with one another, and this is usually transgenerational. Through body focused systemic healing, the client learns how to create healthy relationships through practising healthy boundaries with others, embracing self-care, self-soothing, self-parenting and self-love.

Unconscious Decision Making

Healing during adulthood requires you to shift the childhood perspective that keeps you stuck in life. As one member of the family system, just one piece of the puzzle, clinging to your own narrow perception may contribute to ongoing suffering and struggle. The family system yearns for overall balance and healing. It longs for all the pieces to be found to complete the puzzle. Your family system might be one of those complex thousand-piece jigsaw puzzles, with difficult unusually shaped pieces, or it might resemble a simple twenty-piece puzzle. The family system longs for the flow of love to be restored. It desires unhealthy relationships to shift to be healthy relationships. Some of our beliefs, thoughts and actions are greater than us and greater than our family system. At the collective societal level or the deep ancestral or spiritual levels, you may be unconsciously entangled. Ten percent of the mind is the rational conscious part and the other ninety percent is the unconscious part. A person doesn't tend to consciously choose to harm themselves, to get entangled or to create struggle in their life, so that leaves the unconscious mind to be somehow involved. The unconscious ninety percent of the mind is the main director of the beliefs, thoughts and actions of the human being, not the conscious ten percent. The conscious, rational mind follows the reactive directives of the unconscious mind and sometimes the origins of that information stored in the unconscious mind is very ancient, many generations old. We have autonomic systems in the human body that are still not understood. We are exploring a mysterious realm. We don't have all the answers and to believe otherwise is putting on blinders. We, as human beings, have no idea of the extent and breadth of the talents and capabilities of the unconscious mind. We have no idea how much of our life is predetermined. We have no idea how many of our greatest fears and greatest life challenges were set up by our soul (or deep inner spirit) for our own spiritual and emotional development and growth. Again, acknowledging complicity is vitally important. Your perspective can shift in moments. Many people have no concept of being involved in selecting their own parents to set up these many life challenges. As I have mentioned in many chapters, we benefit when we take a very wide-open systemic perspective to life, to the human journey and to the overall human condition. A sense of deep inner knowing is possible. I know that some people believe otherwise, and they are welcome to their perspective, without judgement on my part. I am relatively new to the exploration of the vast expansiveness of the unconscious mind systemically. I am just learning how the unconscious mind impacts us as the driver in our daily lives. As with many other transgenerational entanglements, incest is an exploration of the unconscious mind, individually and collectively.

Genealogical Incest

Systemically, incest is a great deal more complex than crossing a taboo relationship law. Sometimes the field reveals genealogical incest, referring to sexual relationships between individuals who are energetically close, related by marriage, or raised in the same household but not related by blood ties. However, within most societies there is not a taboo law against marriage or the relationship. These relationships can be very common in some cultures and in some family systems. There may, however, still be a powerful transgenerational energetic impact if you are involved in one of these relationships. These relationships can sometimes be linked to trans-generational trauma flowing from one generation to another. Anne Ancelin Schützenberger, in her book *The Ancestor Syndrome: Transgenerational Psychotherapy and the Hidden Links in the Family System*, discusses some different examples of genealogical incest. She suggests that energetically, these relationships can be too close for some family systems, creating trans-generational issues and persistent conditions such as "cancers, suicides, [and] depressions." [32] Some examples of genealogical incest include:

- Sexual relationship between step-siblings (marrying your new sister or your new brother),

- Sexual relationship between adopted children of different biological parents raised as siblings,

- Sexual relationship between close cousins, and/or,

- Sexual relationship with those connected through marriage such as a sister-in-law, mother-in-law, brother-in-law or father-in-law.

These dynamics are sometimes called double or triple family connections. In my own extended family, a few generations out, there are multiple sisters of one family marrying multiple brothers of another family. I know of an instance where three sisters of one family married three brothers of another family. It happens quite frequently, and it was fairly common in the past in

---

32 Schützenberger, A. A. (1998). *The ancestor syndrome: Transgenerational psychotherapy and the hidden links in the family.* London, UK and New York, NY: Routledge, p. 113.

regions, such as rural communities, where population numbers were low. Some, but not all, of these relationships may create confusion, resentment, feelings of intrusion for some family members and/or identity issues. If you are a woman and you treat your new brother-in-law like he is your brother, then you turn around and marry him, a genealogical incest dynamic may be set up in the family system. If it was your sister that married into his family first, she may resent your intrusion into her family of marriage – the new life she created for herself. Some sisters struggle with sharing their new married name with a sister, given the situation where they both decide to take the common surname of their sibling marital partners.

Genealogical incest may reveal or point to some energetic dynamic that is unresolved in the family system. Genealogical incest may also arise or be significant when there are sexual relationships between individuals with common names. These common names may create identity loss or confusion, or energetic confusion of genealogical position or generations. For example, some mothers-in-law struggle with sharing their married name with a new daughter-in-law. If James Smith marries Susan Brown, and Susan changes her name upon marriage to Susan Smith, or as many cultures traditionally do, Mrs. (James or Susan) Smith, it may highlight a situation where James Smith is unconsciously entangled with his mother, a woman with the same name as his intimate partner. If James Smith marries Carolyn Smith, where they share the same family of origin surname, James may be entangled with the energy of his mother and/or Carolyn with her father.

When a child of one gender is named after the feminine or masculine version of a parent's given name, or the names of ancestors of the opposite gender, such as Roberta named after paternal grandfather Robert, and if Robert happened to experience many traumatic events in his life, Roberta may find she is energetically entangled with her grandfather's unresolved emotional trauma. Genealogical incest may be set up if you marry a woman with the same first or given name as your sister or mother, or, you marry a man with the same first or given name as your brother or father. Both have the potential to create energetic entanglements. There are many examples of relationship dynamics that set up genealogical incest. Unlike family incest, genealogical incest may not be taboo by law, however, it may have a huge energetic impact within certain family systems, creating or pointing to one or several systemic energetic entanglements that seek to be healed, balanced or resolved.

Family

FEBRUARY

Cancer

Written February 4, 2015

I woke up the other day involved in a conversation with cancer. This may sound strange; however, this dialogue was very informative. I thought I would pass on the messages that came forward. Cancer is a symptom or combination of symptoms with a message to deliver to its host. Cancer may be present to support someone in some way or to initiate a shift toward greater energetic and spiritual development and growth. Some days I just wake up knowing what I'm supposed to write about or have an inner understanding about what I am to share with others. I have not been diagnosed with cancer, although, almost three decades ago, when I was much younger, I was treated twice with cryotherapy for pre-cancerous cells. At that time in my life, there was a lot of trauma going on and I was very shutdown emotionally. I was leading my life in a way that was causing potential cancer cells to shift into pre-cancerous cells. We all carry cells that can potentially shift to be cancerous. A malignant soup was forming around the cells of my body. Something needed to change.

When was the last time you heard someone say that they had a friendly conversation with cancer? I suspect the answer is never. The usual reaction of most people to a diagnosis of cancer is fear. This fear is often related to a fear of death. Fear is one of the heaviest emotional energies that we carry in our body. Fear plays various roles in the lives of human beings. It can be a very useful motivator for the human being, for example, to prompt action when life is threatened. Fear shifts the autonomic nervous system of the human being into action. It prompts people to go into fight or flight when a threat is felt. The autonomic nervous system goes on high alert. When there is no longer a threat, and the person has not been required to engage in fight or flight actions, a healthy fight or flight response requires a completion of the movement to occur. If a completion does not occur, the autonomic nervous system remains on full alert charging full speed ahead, and the body holds the fear in the cells of the body. This response can happen with a diagnosis of cancer. This autonomic response is referred to as freeze, as in fight, flight or freeze. When the threat that prompts a fight or flight response goes incomplete, the individual may freeze or experience emotional paralysis. The fear is stored in the body as unresolved emotional trauma.

Human beings would not survive without certain basic fears. "Fearless" individuals often die too soon taking unnecessary risks with their own lives. What we need in our lives is less-fear not fear-less. Regardless of whether you have a serious diagnosis such as cancer or not, it is very helpful to reduce the impact of fear in your life. Fear lies behind many chronic symptoms, conditions and unhealthy behaviours. For more information on systemic healing for chronic symptoms, please read the chapter, *Chronic Illness & Emotional Stress or Trauma*, in Book 1 of this series, *Connect With Your Ancestors*. I encourage anyone with a chronic condition, or anyone who carries symptoms that have no known origin, to read this chapter for any information that might be useful for their situation.

Emotions that Underlie the Symptoms

People diagnosed with cancer usually have a stockpile of unresolved heavy emotions stored in their bodies. Some of these heavy emotions include fear, anger, resentment, regret, shame, guilt, sadness, grief, intolerance, rage, pain, self-denial, hatred, sorrow, embarrassment, worry, self-abandonment, contempt and unhappiness. If this is you, the soup bubbling around the cells of your body is malignant. Another possibility for some situations, if you stepped all over other people to get to where you are in life, or your parents or ancestors did, there may be underlying atonement. If you received a diagnosis of cancer, you may be entangled with or carrying the unresolved transgenerational trauma of your parents and ancestors. You may have unconsciously sacrificed yourself out of deep love and loyalty to your family system to carry this transgenerational trauma or you may have inherited this unresolved trauma. It is important to address this suppressed unresolved emotion to minimize its long-term effect on your life. If a doctor told you that you had elevated levels of certain heavy metals in your body, would you want to do something about it? I suspect the answer is yes. Discovering or admitting that you have heavy emotions in your body is no different. It's time to do something about it. Better yet, be proactive and address the heavy emotions in your body before they make you sick. These heavy emotions aren't just connected to cancer, they are underlying many conditions today. For example, heavy emotions stored in the body are connected to the high levels of obesity being experienced in many regions of the world today. Carrying excess weight has become a huge societal health concern. Ask yourself, in what way is that weight gain emotional? In what way are you attempting to protect your inner Self through weight gain, by creating a barrier or boundary from emotional pain? Along the same line, in what way are you storing heavy emotions in your body as cancer, perhaps carrying much unresolved trauma for others in your family system?

Heightened Stress

A diagnosis of cancer tends to cause stress. During situations of stress, cortisol is released by the adrenal glands. Cortisol is called the stress hormone. Today many people live with chronic stress. It is the reason so many people are diagnosed with adrenal fatigue. To have high levels of cortisol in your blood stream long-term is greatly detrimental to the wellbeing of a human being. It seems to make sense that high stress, high fear and high worry contribute to adrenal fatigue. High levels of cortisol are known to limit learning and memory; impact the immune system; affect bone density; and contribute to weight gain and issues with blood pressure, cholesterol and heart disease. It also contributes to lower life expectancy, less resilience, depression and other mental health concerns.

With a diagnosis of cancer, fear frequently permeates every moment of life, increasing a person's level of stress. Stress and fears create an unhealthy soup around the cells of the body. Living with stress, fear and worry at a heightened level all the time magnifies the malignancy of the soup that surrounds the cells of the body. This is not life giving for the human being. Cancer, autoimmune conditions or other serious diagnoses may be the outcome. I ponder whether it is the diagnosis of cancer, or the fear of cancer created by society, that is more detrimental in the life of a human being.

I believe we have to shift our way of understanding and viewing cancer. I believe there are at least two positive action steps available:

1. We can proactively address the unresolved emotional trauma carried within our bodies, perhaps lessening the possibility of getting certain forms of cancer or other persistent conditions in the first place.

2. We can begin a new dialogue with cancer and let go of the old one. This new conversation requires the development of healthy listening skills. Good listening skills are important for developing relationships and friendships. We can befriend cancer. Cancer carries with it many positive messages for the long-term survival of the person involved and for the balance of their greater family system. We can take the time to listen to these messages and to act upon them for our own highest good. Cancer may let us know what needs to change in our life. We can look at cancer as a benevolent messenger rather than as a scary monster or dragon to be slain.

The Benevolent Messenger

There is another way to look at symptoms and conditions that effect the body. I want to discuss the benevolent messages of cancer. If you have a diagnosis of cancer, you have likely been stewing the cells of your body in unhealthy heavy emotions for a long time. This may be a family pattern that has been passed down from one generation to the next. Cancer doesn't always pass from generation to generation genetically as many are led to believe. It may be passed epigenetically through the emotional expression of the genes. It is frequently the unresolved emotional response patterns that transmit down the family lines. Great grandmother responded emotionally in an unhealthy way, stoically burying her emotional pain and carrying on with life. She may have tragically lost two children to miscarriage, another was stillborn, one died in an accident as a toddler, and she had two sons die in war. Grandmother learned the same emotional response pattern from her mother - just get on with life - and she followed suit, and she passed down the same emotional response pattern to her daughter - your mother. Your mother passed the same emotional response pattern - bury it or sweep it under the carpet - on to you.

Suddenly, or so it appears, cancer arrives knocking at your doorstep. It's time to shift your belief system, your thoughts, your emotional response patterns, and/or your actions. Like many of the symptoms and conditions we experience in our lives, there will tend to be early benevolent messages for us if we pay attention. We need to learn to listen to that inner voice within us – the voice of the unconscious mind. Each symptom delivers a friendly message that our way of being in the world is no longer serving us well. Each message brings with it potential healing. You can be the one to stop this emotional pattern from travelling down another generation.

Listen to Your Inner Voice

When the symptom arrives, you have a choice of shifting or transforming your world, or, digging in your heels with resistance for the fight of your life. If you decide to fight, you may be fighting against your own deep inner Self and your powerful unconscious mind. We frequently hear people refer to their relationship with cancer as a battle. When this occurs, a fight against Self weakens your immune system and your body begins to reject aspects of itself. If we don't listen to our deep inner voice, we are engaged in self-abandonment. It is a rejection of Self. The following questions can be used to understand any symptom or condition that may arrive in your life:

1. When were you diagnosed? What age were you? When did you actually first notice symptoms, even if you ignored them? What age were you?

2. What happened emotionally in the year or so before the symptom appeared? What emotional trauma occurred in your life?

- Did a close family member die or was there a serious accident?

- Did your last child leave home or go off to college?

- Did you have a significant relationship breakup?

- Did you get married?

- Did you move across the country or out of it entirely?

- Did you get a financial windfall or experience financial difficulty?

- Did you have any sort of major change in your life?

- Did you start a new job?

- Did you have a baby?

- Was anyone in your family system unwell?

- Were you impacted by violence or conflict?

- Were you in a major accident?

- Did you lose your job?

3. Did your parents or ancestors experience any of these traumatic life experiences, perhaps at a similar age to your own age at the time of diagnosis?

4. How is the symptom, in this case cancer, serving you? Is it telling you to take care of yourself? Is it telling you that your life is out of balance, that aspects of your life such as your emotions or spiritual well-being are being ignored? Is it telling you that you are taking care of everyone else in your life except for yourself – living in agency? See Book 1 of this Series, *Connect With Your Ancestors*, for more on how to stop living in agency, since living in agency is energy deadening and it is an emotional pattern that travels down from generation to generation. When the energy within your body is deadened, malignancy can step in more easily. Is it telling you that your priorities are out of alignment? Is it telling you that you need to develop healthy relationships with healthy porous boundaries with others, including

the living and the dead? Is it waiting for you to take certain actions in your life – end that unhealthy relationship, quit the job that you hate, connect with your family when there is estrangement, stop working so much, do your emotional healing work around your mother and father, stop living a life filled with regrets, stop worrying about the whole world, stop carrying the burdens of others, get to know your ancestral family system and emotional patterning, etc.

5. If it's a child that is diagnosed with cancer, are the parents willing to do their own deep systemic emotional healing work? What is the child illuminating for the family system?

The Alarm Clock Rings

To understand the messages of cancer, I would suggest you make a list of the things cancer is pushing you to do. Here's a list of some of the key reasons cancer may attempt to get your attention:

It is time to connect to Self. Do you engage in self-abandonment? Do you refuse to care for yourself first? If you are the sort of person that looks after the needs of everyone else but yourself, I am speaking to you. Over and over I read obituaries about individuals who were such givers in their life. They took care of everyone's needs but their own. They sought to fix life for everyone. This is one sure way to become unwell. Many people sacrifice themselves for the wellbeing of others and they pay with their life. When done long-term, this is not exactly a virtue. Those around you may benefit, but you won't. You are meant to find your way back to Self - that deep authentic Self within you. Looking after the needs of others first, sacrificing your own wellbeing, means you are living in agency with others, as mentioned above, and that is energy deadening. You have deemed yourself to be less important than others. A malignant soup is being created for the cells of your body. Looking after the needs of others is sometimes a good excuse or cover up for not wanting to look at your own emotional baggage. When you care for others through your inner emotional woundedness, hoping to find emotional healing, it is energy deadening for you, and sub-sequently, less effective than caring for others through wellness.

It is time for self-care. Cancer wants you to become the centre of your life. If you are the dear sweet individual caring for everyone around you at your own expense, you are denying your own right to health and happiness. This is called self-abandonment. This is an emotional response pattern learned in early life in relationship to your mother. Remember to look back without blame or judgement. This emotional response pattern may be passing from generation to generation. You sacrificed yourself in the womb or in early childhood to keep your mother emotionally well for your own survival. You learned to be a giver to mother rather than learning to take or receive from mother. The healthy flow of love was reversed. Now you find it difficult to receive from others or to accept their help. You became very independent. If you continue to live this same pattern in adulthood, it may harm you and it may kill you. If you continue to live this same pattern throughout your adulthood, you will likely be given another opportunity to listen to your deep inner voice in your next lifetime.

It is time for introspection. Know thyself. Cancer forces you to evaluate your life, encouraging you to go within for introspection and self-analysis. Get a focus on your deep inner dreams and desires and find a way to align your daily life with them. Who are you inside when all the emotional armour is dropped? Are you engaging in self-denial? Do you feel you are unworthy of more, that you are not good enough, that you are not lovable, that you don't deserve to take up space or that you don't have a right to exist? Many of these belief systems relate to the early relationship you developed with your mother in the womb, at or around birth or following birth into early childhood.

It is time to change your life path. Cancer may stop you in your tracks. It lets you know you are heading in a direction that is no longer serving you well. If lets you know that if you continue on this path you may pay the ultimate price with your life.

It is time to take responsibility for your wellbeing. You have to take responsibility for your own life and wellbeing and stop expecting others to do it for you (partners, medical professionals, or family members). Have you experienced a reoccurrence of cancer? This is frequently the outcome when you take medical treatments without addressing the underlying emotional aspects that hold the cancer or any other symptom or condition in your body. Cancer benevolently says, "Even if I am eliminated by radiation, chemo or other treatments – I will return as a symptom in one form or another if the underlying emotional issues that contributed to my creation in the first place are not addressed. I will remain with you until you shift your way of being in the world. I will accompany you until you no longer need my support."

It is time to reconnect to your family system. Cancer pushes you to contemplate what is really important to you in life and to ask for help. It draws your family members and friends in close to you. Are you the black sheep of the family system? Are you estranged from your family? Did you move a great distance away to intentionally separate from your family? Sometimes cancer illuminates someone missing or excluded in the family system, a parent or ancestor, or a child that died in the womb or otherwise too soon. It may be time to emotionally welcome in anyone missing or excluded from the family system, including you.

It is time to overhaul yourself emotionally. It pushes you to address the heavy emotions stored in your body – fear, anger, resentment, intolerance, regret, shame, guilt, self-abandonment, hatred, sadness, grief, rage, pain, sorrow, contempt and unhappiness or any other heavy emotion. What heavy emotions are you storing inside that need to be released? It may be time to explore new positive and lighter emotions, such as joy, happiness, hope, awe, curiosity, gratitude and contentment, living through love rather than fear, to create new emotional response patterns and strategies.

It is time to set priorities. Are you ignoring any aspect of your life? Are you balancing your emotional, physical, spiritual, mental, psychological, financial and relationship wellbeing? It may be time to focus on the aspects of your life that have been ignored for far too long.

It is time to create a healthy boundary. Cancer may arrive to serve as a boundary for you. Do you have either no energy boundary with others, allowing them to walk all over you, or do you have a boundary so un-porous and rigid that you keep everyone away?

It is time to address your inner wounds. Any wound that is left to fester will eventually get infected and threaten your life. The unresolved emotional wounds of the child within you surround the cells of your body making you unwell. Have you addressed the emotional trauma experienced in this lifetime? It may have occurred in childhood, and it may be conscious or unconscious. Did you unconsciously sacrifice yourself in the womb or in early childhood to care for your mother's emotional wellbeing? Do you have an attachment wound with your mother and/or father? Did you attempt to hold the relationship of your mother and father together in any way? Are you the family mediator or peacekeeper? Are you the family scapegoat, unconsciously holding all the family secrets or all the things that go wrong in the family system? The family dynamic behind scapegoating can be, "better you than me." Are you energetically entangled with any other member of your family system, living or dead? Do you carry unresolved transgenerational emotional wounds for your family system? Have you appropriately mourned any children of your own that did not come to life or that died too soon?

It is time to surrender to vulnerability. Are you inflexible? Are you attempting to control everything in your life? Human beings will ultimately fail if they continue this behaviour because it is unattainable. You can take charge of things in your life; however, you can't control your life. You can die attempting to control your life. This inflexibility is harmful to your overall wellbeing. Perfectionism is another unattainable state of being that sets you up for feelings of failure. If you insist on following a path toward perfection, you are only harming yourself and creating your own unwellness.

It is time to soften the emotional armour. Are you judgmental? Are you living in a black and white world without any shades of gray? Do you insist on always being right? Are you closed-minded? Are you self-righteous with others? Do you feel hatred for those different from you? Are you afraid to explore the world? Are you living through fear rather than love? Do you feel superior to others? Are you racist? Are you xenophobic? Do you often reveal your prejudice? Have you stepped all over others to get to the top? Do you treat those you consider beneath you in a poor manner? Do you live through a narrow childhood perspective of life that needs to expand to take in the big picture? It may be time to learn new ways of being in the world and to develop emotional maturity.

It is time to engage with the energetic collective. Do you deny your existence as a spiritual being? Have you strayed or separated from the spiritual and emotional development goals you desired to achieve in this lifetime? Do you support individualism to the extreme, unable to experience unity? Do you feel disconnected? Do you lack a spiritual sense of connection to a higher collective energy that is more expansive than yourself? Do you fail to see yourself as part of a greater whole? Do you feel you are accountable to no one or no thing? Are you independent to a fault? Do you ignore or deny the mystery of life or anything that cannot be seen or proven empirically? It may be time to explore life and the greater world around you in a new expansive way.

It is time to balance the inner masculine and feminine. Cancer can indicate that you have rejected either your inner masculine or your inner feminine. Do you reject your mother, your father or both? That gives you a quick assessment of where you stand with regard to rejecting aspects of Self. Do you reject the fifty percent of Self that is related to mother or the fifty percent of Self that is related to father, or do you reject both, and effectively reject one hundred percent of Self? It is tough to be well when you reject yourself entirely. Cancers of the reproductive or sexual organs are common and related to your wellbeing on this spectrum:

Men: Prostate cancer – Do you live through fear rather than love? A good example here that is known universally is the right of United States' citizens to bear arms. Do you support the right to bear arms out of fear that your own government does not have your best interests at heart? That is a good example of living through fear. Another example, if you watch the news intently every day you may be living through fear. Looking at the family system, have you spent years consciously or unconsciously rejecting your father? Are you closer to your mother than your father? Does your mother stand energetically in the way of you getting closer to your father, consciously or unconsciously, desiring her own emotional needs to be met by you and refusing to step back energetically to allow the relationship with father to occur? Are you becoming more like your father every day and does this feel like a bad thing? Do you feel disconnected from the long line of strong effective male ancestors behind you? If you don't know much about them you are disconnected. Are the events of your family's ancestral life journeys problematic for you? Is there gender bias against boys and men in your family system - they are the weaker sex - needing a good woman to care for them? Are you homophobic - rigidly rejecting the variations on the spectrum of sexuality and gender? These questions will get you started on a journey to address unresolved emotional trauma that relates to the balance of the masculine and feminine energies within you.

Women: Do you live through fear rather than love? Breast cancer, cervical cancer, ovarian cancer – Have you spent years consciously or unconsciously rejecting your mother? Are you emotionally close to your mother? Are you too close to your mother - her confidante or best friend? Are you closer to your father than your mother? Are you becoming more like your mother every day and does this feel like a bad thing? Do you feel disconnected from the long line of strong effective female ancestors behind you? If you don't know much about them you are disconnected. Are the events of your family's ancestral life journeys problematic for you? Is there gender bias against girls and women in your family system - boys are favoured - it's not safe to be a girl - girls can't do it as well as boys - a girl needs to find a good man to care for her? Are you homophobic - rejecting the variations on the spectrum of sexuality and gender? These questions will get you started on a journey to address unresolved emotional trauma that relates to the balance of the masculine and feminine energies within you.

The Unwelcome Visitor

I know that people tend to believe that a diagnosis of cancer is a shock - that it arrives unexpectedly. I also know that many people dislike unexpected visitors. If we are really truthful with ourselves, cancer does not tend to arrive unexpectedly. Cancer grows in the body over long periods of time. Cancer usual gives plenty of warning - attempting to communicate with you through many other symptoms of unwellness. There may be many emotional symptoms that manifest over time. There may be physical symptoms as well. Too often, the symptoms go unheeded, and the inner voice attempting to help you, or to get you to change in some way, is ignored or silenced. Cancer arrived and suddenly it seemed a little more important to pay attention to the symptoms.

Cancer is a wake-up call. Sometimes it is the final wake-up call. It may be letting you know that you have hit the snooze button of life once too many times. It tells you that it is TIME!! It may also tell you that you have taken too long to respond and there may be a consequence. We all carry cells in our body that can become cancerous. Why does it happen to some and not to others? I once worked with a lovely young woman who listened to the messages of her cancer symptoms and one day she gave me the answer. She said, "People with cancer are carrying a lot of stuff - sometimes it's a lot of pain that belongs to others. I realize I worked hard to get cancer over a long period of time. I let people dump all their issues on me and I carried it for them." Through introspection, listening to the messages of the cancer, this young woman had gained great insight and wisdom. For her life journey, it was a reoccurrence of cancer in a much more powerful form, after neglecting to shift her way of life and way of being in the world for far too long. She gained much through her systemic healing journey for her life and her family system.

I encourage you to take the time to listen to the messages of cancer, or any other body symptom or condition you may have. I encourage you to figure out what the symptom is saying specifically to you. Better yet, proactively shift the unresolved emotional trauma that is suppressed in your body. Bring it out into the open to be expressed and processed before it creates unwellness, or an unhealthy malignant soup around the cells of your body. Cancer is a symptom of a family system! We don't become unwell in isolation and we don't heal in isolation. Cancer is meant to be addressed systemically through the context of our family system. How is your connection to your family system and to your ancestors? Now is the time to transform whatever needs to be transformed, and to begin living life fully!! It is time to shift all the unhealthy relationships into healthy relationships. Much of what I have shared in this chapter was learned through that early morning conversation with cancer. It blended together with what I had learned through many systemic and family constellations and body focused integrative approaches to wellbeing.

Family

FINAL REFLECTION

Expanding the awareness and use of systemic healing as it pertains to Self, family, community or society is my goal. We are living in an amazing time when the silenced are finding their voices and what was silenced is finally being heard. It is my hope that you have found one or more of these topics of discussion interesting and perhaps relevant to your own life. Some controversial subjects such as Patriarchy, Incest, Abortion, Residential Schools and Cancer were explored for the expansion of us all. It was important to bring them out into the light for a closer look. In order to understand family dynamics, it's often important to discuss some difficult subjects. So much has been silenced in the past. I hope you found these topics and others thought provoking.

I have learned that each family member experiences the world and their family system in a different way. Each of us will have a different perspective on these topics and I encourage you to really get a sense of how you feel about them. You certainly don't have to agree with what I have said. If there is one thing I have learned through working with clients and experiencing systemic and family constellations, it is that reality can be very challenging and surreal at times. It is vital to look back at what was and what is, without whitewashing the real world. When we embrace radical inclusion, not only do we include all family members who are missing, excluded, forgotten, shunned, cast out or excommunicated, we also delve into all of the topics that have been previously deemed taboo by families and societies.

I encourage you to read the chapters in Book 1 of this series, *Connect With Your Ancestors*, and Book 2 of this Series, *Let Your Tears Flow*, if you haven't already done so, to expand your vocabulary and knowledge around systemic healing. They cover a whole range of different systemic healing subjects. Be sure to watch for the fourth book to be published in this Series in the near future. As you *Connect With Your Ancestors* in a strong emotional way, and *Let Your Tears Flow*, by connecting with your emotional body, feelings and strong inner voice, you will be ready to *Step into the Light.* You will be well along in your journey toward transforming the transgenerational trauma of your family tree. Your worldview will be expanding and your sense of how you fit into your family system and the world around you will be clearer. Any narrow perspective you may have had will be rapidly broadening, opening you to interact and interconnect with all other perspectives. Any concern you may have in life will no longer feel individual or centred only on you, as you look to your greater family and community systems for answers, guidance and resolution. Systemic healing is a fascinating and challenging way to look at each obstacle that crosses your path. Embracing a body focus to all your concerns will bring immense transformation into your life. You begin to understand the origins of emotional response strategies and patterns that have kept you stuck or in repetitive life patterns for many years, or perhaps your whole lifetime. You open up to new peaceful possibilities for your life and come closer to finding inner peace. I encourage you to utilize systemic constellations as one approach for gaining insight or a new inner image for your systemic healing. Systemic constellations connect you to the greater systemic field that surrounds you, and initiate the inner movements of your soul and your body that bring about healing for Self, family and community.

SOME SUGGESTED READING

Transgenerational Trauma

Bar-On, D. (1995). *Fear and hope: Three generations of the Holocaust.* Cambridge, MA: Harvard University Press.

Danieli, Y. (Ed.). (2010). *International handbook of multigenerational legacies of trauma.* New York & London: Plenum Press. (Original work published 1998)

Hart, B. (Ed.). *Peacebuilding in traumatized societies.* Lanham, MD: University Press of America.

Lieberman, S. (1979). *Transgenerational family therapy.* London, UK: Croom Helm.

Maté, G. (2008). *In the realm of hungry ghosts: Close encounters with addictions.* Toronto, ON: Vintage Canada.

Moser, K. (2014). *Transgenerational trauma in the Northern Ireland context: A social work perspective.* Saarbrücken, Germany: Akademikervertag.

Mucci, Clara. (2013). *Beyond individual and collective trauma: Intergenerational transmission, psychoanalytic treatment, and the dynamics of forgiveness.* London, UK: Karnac.

Muid, O. (2004). *"...Then I lost my spirit": An analytic essay on transgenerational trauma theory as applied to oppressed people of color nations.* Retrieved from ProQuest on September 12, 2015 from

https://ezproxy.royalroads.ca/login?url=http://search.proquest.com/
docview/305061635?accountid=8056

Roberto, L. G. (1992). *Transgenerational family therapies.* New York &
London: The Guilford Press.

Schwab, G. (2010). *Haunting legacies: Violent histories and transgenerational trauma.* New York: Columbia University Press.

Sigal, J. and Weinfeld, M. (1989). *Trauma and rebirth: Intergenerational effects of the Holocaust.* New York: Praeger.

St. Just, A. (2008). *A question of balance: A systemic approach to understanding and resolving trauma.* USA: Anngwyn St. Just.

St. Just, A. (2012). *Trauma: Time, space and fractals: A systemic perspective on individual, social and global trauma.* USA: Anngwyn St. Just.

St. Just, A. (2013). *Waking to the sound of thunder: Trauma and the human condition II.* USA: Anngwyn St. Just.

St. Just, A. (2014). *At paradigm's edge: Trauma and the human condition III.* USA: Anngwyn St. Just.

Tick, E. (2014). *Warrior's return: Restoring the soul after war.* Boulder, Colorado: Sounds True.

Weinstein, A. D. (2013). Consequences of maternal traumatic stress experience. In M. J. Shea (Ed.), *Biodynamic craniosacral therapy (Vol. 5)*. Berkley, CA: North Atlantic Books.

Yehuda, R., Schmeidler, J., Elkin, A., Wilson, G. S., Siever, L., Binder-Brynes, K., Wainberg, M., & Aferiot, D. (2010). Phenomenology and psychobiology of the intergenerational response to trauma. In Y. Danieli (Ed.), *International handbook of multigenerational legacies of trauma*. New York & London: Plenum Press.

Yehuda, R., Mulherin Engel, S., Brand, S. R., Seckl, J., Marcus, S. M., & Berkowitz, G. S. (2005). Transgenerational effects of posttraumatic stress disorder in babies of mothers exposed to the World Trade Center attacks during pregnancy. *The Journal of Clinical Endocrinology & Metabolism, 90*(7), 4115-4118. Doi:10.1210/jc.2005-0550.

Body Focused Trauma Approaches

Hellier, L. and LaPierre, A. (2012). *Healing developmental trauma: How early trauma affects self-regulation, self-image, and the capacity for relationship*. Berkeley, CA: North Atlantic Books.

Levine, P. A. (2005). *Healing trauma*. Boulder, CO: Sounds True, Inc.

Levine, P. A. (2010). *In an unspoken voice: How the body releases trauma and restores goodness*. Berkeley, CA: North Atlantic Books.

Levine, P. A. (2015). *Trauma and memory: Brain and body in a search for the living past*. Berkeley, CA: North Atlantic Books.

Lifton, R. J. (1988). Understanding the traumatized self: Imagery, symbolization, and transformation. In J. P. Wilson, Z. Harel, & B. Kahana (Eds.), *Human adaptation to extreme stress: From the Holocaust to Vietnam* (pp. 7-31). New York, NY: Plenum Press.

Lipton, B. H. (2008). *The biology of belief: Unleashing the power of consciousness, matter & miracles.* New York City, NY: Hay House.

Pert, C. B. (1997). *Molecules of emotion: The science behind mind-body medicine.* New York, NY: Scribner.

Robertson, P. K. (2017). *Let your tears flow: Transforming the transgenerational trauma of your family tree.* Pennsauken, NJ: Peaceful Possibilities Press.

Robertson, P. K. (2018). *Connect with your ancestors: Transforming the transgenerational trauma of your family tree.* Pennsauken, NJ: Peaceful Possibilities Press.

Rothschild, B. (2002). *The body remembers: The psychophysiology of trauma and trauma treatment.* New York & London: W. W. Norton & Company.

Siegel, D. J. (2010). *About interpersonal neurobiology.* Retrieved October 17, 2016 from http://www.drdansiegel.com/about/interpersonal_neurobiology/

Siegel, D. J. (2012). *The developing mind, second edition: How relationships and the brain interact to shape who we are.* New York, NY: The Guilford Press.

Genosociograms

McGoldrick, M., Gerson, R., & Petry, S. (2008). *Genograms: Assessment and intervention (3rd ed.)*. New York & London: W. W. Norton & Company, Inc.

Schützenberger, A. A. (1998). *The ancestor syndrome: Transgenerational psychotherapy and the hidden links in the family*. London, UK and New York, NY: Routledge.

Systems Approaches

Capra, F., & Luisi, P. L. (2014). *The systems view of life: A unifying vision*. Cambridge, UK: Cambridge University Press.

Laszlo, E. (1996). *The systems view of the world: A holistic vision for our time*. Cresskill, NJ: Hampton Press.

Systemic Constellations

Beaumont, H. (2012). *Toward a spiritual psychotherapy: Soul as a dimension of experience*. Berkeley, CA: North Atlantic Books.

Booth Cohen, D. (2009). *I carry your heart in my heart: Family constellations in prison*. Heidelberg, Germany: Carl-Auer-Systeme Verlag.

Broughton, V. (2010). *In the presence of many: Reflections on constellations emphasising the individual context*. United Kingdom: Green Balloon Publishing.

Franke, U. (2003). *In my mind's eye: Family constellations in individual therapy and counselling* (Trans. C. Beaumont*)*. Heidelberg, Germany: Carl-Auer.

Hausner, S. (2011). *Even if it costs me my life.* Santa Cruz, CA: GestaltPress.

Hellinger, B., Weber, G., & Beaumont, H. (1998). *Love's hidden symmetry: What makes love work in relationships.* Phoenix, AR: Zeig, Tucker & Co.

Hellinger, B. (1999). *Acknowledging what is: Conversations with Bert Hellinger* (Trans. C. Beaumont). Phoenix, Arizona: Zeig, Tucker & Co., Inc.

Hellinger, B. (2001). *Love's own truths: Bonding and balancing in close relationships* (M. Oberli-Turner & H. Beaumont, Trans.). Phoenix, AZ: Zeig, Tucker & Theisen.

Hellinger, B. (2003). *To the heart of the matter: Brief therapies.* Heidelberg, Germany: Carl-Auer-Systeme Verlag.

Hellinger, B. (2003). *Farewell: Family constellations with descendants of victims and perpetrators.* (C. Beaumont, Trans.). Heidelberg, Germany: Carl-Auer-Systeme Verlag.

Hellinger, B. (2003). *Rachel weeping for her children: Family constellations in Israel.* Heidelberg, Germany: Carl-Auer-Systeme Verlag.

Hellinger, B. (2006). *No waves without the ocean: Experiences and thoughts* (J. ten Herkel & S. Tombleson, Trans.). Heidelberg, Germany: Carl-Auer-Systeme Verlag.

Hellinger, B. (2009). *Peace begins in the soul* (Trans. A. Schenk, Revised S. Tucker). Bischofswiesen, Germany: Hellinger Publications.

Hellinger, B. (2010). *Rising in love: A philosophy of being.* Bischofswiesen, Germany: Hellinger Publications.

Lynch, J. E., & Tucker, S. (Eds.). (2005). *Messengers of healing: The family constellations of Bert Hellinger through the eyes of a new generation of practitioners.* Phoenix, AZ: Zeig, Tucker & Theisen, Inc.

Mahr, A. (1999). "Das wissende feld: Familienaufstellung als geistig energetisches heilen" ["The knowing field: Family constellations as mental and energetic healing"]. In *Geistiges heilen für eine neue zeit* [*Intellectual cures for a new time*]. Heidelberg, Germany: Kösel Verlag.

Manné, J. (2009). *Family constellations: A practical guide to uncovering the origins of family conflict.* Berkeley, CA: North Atlantic Books.

Mason Boring, F. (2004). *Feather medicine, walking in Shoshone dreamtime: A family system constellation.* USA: Francesca Mason Boring.

Mason Boring, F. (2012). *Connecting to our ancestral past: Healing through family constellations, ceremony, and ritual.* Berkeley, CA: North Atlantic Books.

Mason Boring, F. (2013). *Family systems constellations: And other systems constellations adventures: A transformational journey.* USA: Franscesca Mason Boring.

Mason Boring, F., & Sloan, K. E. (Eds.) (2013). *Returning to membership in Earth community: Systemic constellations with nature.* Pagosa Springs, CO: Stream of Experience Productions.

Payne, J. L. (2005). *The healing of individuals, families, and nations: Trans-generational healing & family constellations.* Findhorn, Forres, Scotland: Findhorn Press.

Payne, J. L. (2006). *The language of the soul: Trans-generational healing & family constellations.* Findhorn, Forres, Scotland: Findhorn Press.

Payne, J. L. (2007). *The presence of the soul: Transforming your life through soul awareness.* Findhorn, Forres, Scotland: Findhorn Press.

Reddy, M. (2012). *Health, happiness, & family constellations: How ancestors, family systems, and hidden loyalties shape your life – and what you can do about it.* Kimberton, PA: ReddyWorks.

Ruppert, F. (2008). *Trauma, bonding & family constellations: Understand and healing injuries of the soul.* Frome, Somerset, UK: Green Balloon Publishing.

Schmidt, J. B. (2006). *Inner navigation: Trauma healing and constellational process work as navigational tools for the evolution of your true self.* Hamburg, Germany: Johannes Benedikt Schmidt.

Sparrer, I. (2007). *Miracle, solution and system: Solution-focused systemic structural constellations for therapy and organisational change.* Cheltenham, UK: SolutionsBooks.

Ulsamer, B. (2003). *The art and practice of family constellations: Leading family constellations as developed by Bert Hellinger* (Trans. C. Beaumont). Heidelberg, Germany: Carl-Auer-Systeme.

Ulsamer, B. (2005). *The healing power of the past: A new approach to healing family wounds: The systemic therapy of Bert Hellinger.* Nevada City, CA: Underwood Books.

van Kampenhout, D. (2001). *Images of the soul: The working of the soul in shamanic rituals and family constellations.* Phoenix, Arizona: Zeig, Tucker & Theisen, Inc.

van Kampenhout, D. (2008). *The tears of the ancestors: Victims and perpetrators in the tribal soul.* Phoenix, Arizona: Zeig, Tucker & Theisen, Inc.

Wolynn, M. (2016). *It didn't start with you: How inherited family trauma shapes who we are and how to end the cycle.* New York, NY: Viking.

Epigenetics

Anway, M. D., Cupp, A. S., et al. (2005). Epigenetic transgenerational actions of endocrine disruptors and male fertility. *Science, 308,* 1466-1469.

Bernstein, B. E., Meissner, A., & Lander, E. S. (2007). The mammalian epigenome. *Cell, 128,* 669-681. doi: 10.1016/j.cell.2007.01.033.

Bird, A. (2007). Introduction perceptions of epigenetics [Abstract]. *Nature*, *447*, 396-398. doi:10.1038/nature05913.

Bond, D. M. & Pedersen, C. A. (2007). Passing the message on: Inheritance of epigenetic traits. *Trends Plant Science*, 12(4), 211-216.

Cao-Lei, L., Massart, R., Suderman, M. J., Machnes, Z., Elgbeili, G., Laplante, D. P., Szyf, M., and King, S. (2014). DNA Methylation signatures triggered by prenatal maternal stress exposure to a natural disaster: Project ice storm. *PLoS ONE*, *9*, 9: e107653 doi: 10.1371/journal.pone.0107653.

Carey, N. (2012). *The epigenetics revolution: How modern biology is rewriting our understanding of genetics, disease, and inheritance*. New York: Columbia University Press.

Church, D. (2008). *The genie in your genes: Epigenetic medicine and the new biology of intention*. Santa Rosa, CA: Energy Psychology Press.

Conradt, E., Lester, B. M., Appleton, A. A., Armstrong, D. A., and Marsit, C. J. (2013). The role of DNA methylation of NR3C1 and 11β-HSD2 and exposure to maternal mood disorder in utero on newborn neurobehavior. *Epigenetics*, *8*(12). doi:10.4161/epi.26634.

Delaval, K. & Feil, R. (2004). Epigenetic regulation of mammalian genomic imprinting. *Current Opinion in Genetics and Development*, *14*, 2, 188-195.

Egger, G., Liang, G., et al. (2004). Epigenetics in human disease and prospects for epigenetic therapy. *Nature*, *429*, 457-463.

Francis, R. C. (2011). *Epigenetics: How environment shapes our genes.* New York & London: W. W. Norton & Company.

Franklin, T. B. (2009). *Study of the mechanisms of transgenerational inheritance of behavioural alterations induced by early stress in mice.* Unpublished Doctoral Dissertation. Dalhousie University, Halifax, NS.

Franklin, T. B. & Mansuy, I. M. (2010). Epigenetic inheritance in mammals: Evidence for the impact of adverse environmental effects. *Neurobiology of Disease, 39,* 61-65.

Goldberg, A. D., Allis, C. D., & Bernstein, E. (2007). Epigenetics: A landscape takes shape. *Cell, 128,* 635-638. doi: 10.1016/j.cell.2007.02.006.

Gräff, J., Franklin, T. B., & Mansuy, I. M. (2011). Epigenetics of Brain Disorders. *Handbook of epigenetics* (pp. 553-567). Amsterdam, The Netherlands: Elsevier. doi:10.1016/B978-0-12-375709-8.00034-4.

Harper, L. V. (2005). Epigenetic inheritance and the intergenerational transfer of experience. *Psychological Bulletin, 131*(3), 340-60.

Iversen, A. C., Fear, N. T., et al. (2007). Influence of childhood adversity on health among male UK military personnel. *British Journal of Psychiatry, 191,* 506-511.

Jablonka, E., & Raz, G. (2009). Transgenerational epigenetic inheritance: Prevalence, mechanisms, and implications for the study of heredity and evolution. *The Quarterly Review of Biology Journal, 84*(2), 131-176. PubMed 19606595. Retrieved from http://www.ncbi.nlm.nih.gov/pubmed/19606595.

Jaffee, S. R., Moffitt, T. E., et al. (2002). Differences in early childhood risk factors for juvenile-onset and adult-onset depression. *Archives of General Psychiatry, 59*(3), 215-222).

Jirtle, R. L. & Skinner, M. K. (2007). Environmental epigenomics and disease susceptibility. *Nature Reviews Genetics, 8*(4), 253-62.

Manassis, K. & Bradley, S. (1995). Behavioural inhibition, attachment and anxiety in children of mothers with anxiety disorders. *Canadian Journal of Psychiatry, 40*(2), 87-92.

McGowan, P. O., Sasaki, A., et al. (2009). Epigenetic regulation of the glucocorticoid receptor in human brain associates with childhood abuse. *Nature Neuroscience, 12*(3), 342-348.

Meaney, M. J. (2001). Maternal care, gene expression, and the transmission of individual differences in stress reactivity across generations. *Annual Review Neuroscience, 24*, 1161-1192.

Merikangas, K. R., Swendsen, J. D., et al. (1998). Psychopathology and temperament in parents and offspring: Results of a family study. *Journal of Affective Disorders, 51*(1), 63-74.

Nilsson, E. E., Anway, M. D., et al. (2008). Transgenerational epigenetic effects of the endocrine disruptor vinclozolin on pregnancies and female adult onset disease. *Reproduction, 135*(5), 713-21.

Pembrey, M. E., Bygren, L. O., et al. (2006). Sex-specific, male-line transgenerational responses in humans. *European Journal of Human Genetics, 14*(2), 159-66.

Petronis, A., Gottesman, II, et al. (2003). Monozygotic twins exhibit numerous epigenetic differences: Clues to twin discordance? *Schizophrenia Bulletin, 29*(1), 169-178.

Phillips, R. G. & LeDoux, J. E. (1992). Differential contribution of amygdala and hippocampus to cued and contextual fear conditioning. *Behavioral Neuroscience,* 106(2), 274-285.

Richardson, B. C. (2002). Role of DNA methylation in the regulation of cell function: Autoimmunity, aging and cancer. *Journal Nutrition, 8 Supplement,* 2401S-2405S.

Rikhye, K., Tyrka, A. R., et al. (2008). Interplay between childhood maltreatment, parental bonding, and gender effects: Impact on quality of life. *Child Abuse Neglect Journal,* 32(1), 19-34.

Shamir-Essakow, G., Ungerer, J. A., et al. (2005). Attachment, behavioral inhibition, and anxiety in preschool children. *Journal of Abnormal Childhood Psychology, 33*(2), 133-143.

Skinner, M. K. (2008). What is an epigenetic transgenerational phenotype? F3 or F2. *Reproductive Toxicology, 25*(1), 2-6.

Sroufe, L.A., 2002. From infant attachment to promotion of adolescent autonomy: Prospective, longitudinal data on the role of parents. In S. L. R. J. G. Borkowski, M. Bristol-Power (Eds.), *Parenting and the child's world: Influences on ... intellectual and socio-emotional development* (pp. 187-202). Mahwah, NJ: Erlbaum.

Susser, M. & Stein, Z. (1994). Timing in prenatal nutrition: A reprise of the Dutch famine study. *Nutrition Review, 52*(3), 84-94.

Trasler, J. M. (2006). Gamete imprinting: Setting epigenetic patterns for the next generation. *Reproduction, Fertility and Development, 18*(1-2), 63-69.

Tsankova, N., Renthal, W., et al. (2009). Epigenetic regulation in psychiatric disorders. *Nature Reviews Neuroscience, 8*(5), 355-367.

van Vliet, J., Oates, N. A., et al. (2007). Epigenetic mechanisms in the context of complex diseases. *Cellular Molecular Life Sciences, 64*(12), 1531-1538.

Veenema, A. H., Blume, A., et al. (2006). Effects of early life stress on adult male aggression and hypothalamic vasopressin and serotonin. *European Journal of Neuroscience, 24*(6), 1711-1720.

Wallach, J. D., Lan, M., & Schrauzer, G. N. (2014). *Epigenetics: The death of the genetic theory of disease transmission.* New York, NY: SelectBooks.

Weaver, I. C., Cervoni, N. Champagne, F. A., D'Alessio, A. C., Sharma, S., Seckl, J. R., Dymov, S., Szuf, M., & Meaney, M. J. (2004). Epigenetic programming by maternal behavior. *Natural Neuroscience, 7,* 847-854.

Weaver, I. C., Champagne, F. A., Brown, S. E., Dymov, S., Sharma, S., Meaney, M. J., & Szyf, M. (2005). Reversal of maternal programming of stress responses in adult offspring through methyl supplementation: Altering epigenetic marking later in life. *Journal of Neuroscience, 25,* 11045-11054.

Weissman, M. M., Leckman, J. F., et al. (1984). Depression and anxiety disorders in parents and children. Results from the Yale family study. *Archives of General Psychiatry, 41*(9), 845-852.

Wilson, A. S., Power, B. E., et al. (2007). DNA hypmethylation and human diseases. *Biochimica et Biophysica Acta, 1775(1),* 138-162.

Wilson, V. L. & Jones, P. A. (1983). DNA methylation decreases in aging but not in immortal cells. *Science, 200,* 4601, 1055-1057.

Xing, Y., Shi, S., et al. (2007). Evidence for transgenerational transmission of epigenetic tumor susceptibility in Drosophila. *PLoS Genetics, 3*(9), 1598-1606.

Yang, J., Li, W., et al. (2006). Enriched environment treatment counteracts enhanced addictive and depressive-like behavior induced by prenatal chronic stress. *Brain Research,* 1125(1), 132-137.

Zamenhof, S., van Marthens, E., et al. (1971). DNA (cell number) in neonatal brain: Second generation (F2) alteration by maternal (F0) dietary protein restriction. *Science, 172,* 985, 850-851.

INDEX

A

abandonment 14, 51, 52, 71, 73, 74, 75, 98, 106, 107, 114, 118, 124, 126
Aboriginal Healing Foundation 12, 14, 29
abortion 5, 46, 79, 80, 81, 82, 83, 84, 85, 87, 88, 89, 90, 91, 92, 93, 94, 103, 129,
　　132, 144, 187
abundance 44
abuse 15, 16, 17, 23, 25, 87, 134, 157, 160, 162, 163, 164, 165, 166, 200, 201
accidents 103, 136, 178
acknowledgement 1, 4, 8, 22, 26, 32, 79, 80, 81, 83, 84, 86, 88, 90, 91, 92, 94, 105,
　　111, 116, 117, 120, 126, 127, 129, 134, 137, 141, 158, 162, 163, 166
acknowledging what is 156, 158, 194
action 1, 5, 16, 22, 26, 28, 29, 33, 34, 37, 38, 40, 47, 48, 67, 68, 71, 79, 81, 87, 92,
　　102, 113, 125, 133, 145, 150, 158, 159, 162, 166, 167, 173, 176, 177, 179,
　　197
addiction 15, 17, 37, 47, 64, 80, 100, 129, 134, 160, 189, 203
adoption 9, 60, 80, 82, 97, 103, 107, 124, 129, 144, 169
adrenal symptoms 44, 175
adults 23, 42, 48, 51, 52, 60, 98, 99, 103, 111, 114, 116, 117, 118, 120, 122, 123,
　　126, 128, 133, 134, 146, 148, 149, 159, 163, 165, 166, 200, 202
advancement 1, 2, 3, 74, 145, 165
agency, living in 44, 61, 77, 101, 116, 130, 135, 178
aggression 17, 159, 202
aging 126, 201, 203
agreements 151, 157
alienation 17, 98
alone 49, 51, 56, 76, 107, 115, 160
Anaya, J. 27
ancestors 187
Ancestor Syndrome 169
ancestral v, vi, 2, 4, 8, 28, 37, 39, 45, 47, 57, 62, 67, 70, 83, 94, 99, 102, 112, 120,
　　129, 134, 136, 143, 144, 150, 152, 158, 160, 161, 163, 168, 169, 170, 174,
　　178, 179, 181, 182, 184, 186, 187, 193, 195, 196, 197
ancestral emotional trauma 37, 129, 158, 160
ancient wisdom 3, 4
anger 4, 15, 26, 34, 37, 43, 48, 60, 62, 89, 111, 122, 130, 159, 174, 181
anniversaries 36, 136
anxiety 43, 50, 70, 90, 130, 159, 200, 201, 203
arthritis 43, 129, 130
assimilation v, 12, 22, 24
atonement 127, 161
attachment 3, 60, 66, 82, 98, 99, 106, 107, 109, 114, 119, 126, 165, 182, 200, 201

E

family constellations iv, 6, 26, 35, 39, 45, 55, 66, 67, 69, 70, 81, 84, 91, 93, 94, 108,
112, 115, 129, 138, 139, 141, 143, 145, 147, 148, 149, 150, 152, 155, 156,
157, 158, 159, 160, 161, 162, 163, 164, 165, 166, 186, 187, 188, 193, 194,
195, 196, 197
family friend 164
family member 10, 17, 33, 34, 36, 38, 45, 46, 49, 57, 63, 67, 80, 88, 92, 94, 100,
107, 120, 136, 144, 148, 158, 160, 161, 163, 164, 167, 170, 178, 181, 187
family secrets 81, 103, 182
family system 4, 5, 8, 9, 10, 13, 16, 31, 33, 34, 35, 38, 39, 45, 47, 50, 51, 55, 57, 58,
61, 66, 67, 79, 80, 81, 82, 83, 85, 86, 88, 89, 90, 91, 92, 93, 94, 99, 100, 103,
105, 106, 111, 112, 115, 116, 117, 120, 123, 125, 126, 127, 128, 129, 130,
131, 135, 136, 139, 141, 142, 143, 144, 145, 147, 148, 149, 150, 151, 152,
155, 156, 157, 158, 159, 160, 161, 163, 164, 166, 167, 169, 170, 171, 174,
176, 179, 181, 182, 184, 186, 187, 195, 196
family tree 188
family violence 15
fate 108, 115, 129, 135
father 9, 18, 19, 25, 37, 45, 53, 61, 66, 79, 80, 82, 84, 85, 88, 89, 91, 92, 93, 94, 97,
99, 100, 104, 107, 113, 119, 122, 124, 128, 132, 134, 135, 137, 140, 141, 142,
144, 145, 147, 148, 151, 152, 155, 158, 160, 162, 163, 169, 170, 171, 179,
182, 183, 184
fear 2, 4, 5, 10, 15, 17, 18, 24, 35, 46, 50, 51, 54, 56, 57, 62, 89, 90, 100, 102, 116,
129, 132, 138, 147, 158, 159, 165, 168, 173, 174, 175, 181, 183, 189, 199,
201
fear tactics 24
fear the same fate 90
fear they will die 90
feelings 10, 14, 15, 52, 54, 57, 59, 60, 61, 64, 70, 71, 72, 74, 75, 92, 99, 100, 102,
105, 107, 118, 124, 126, 131, 136, 152, 157, 159, 170, 182, 187
female 84, 132, 145, 155, 165, 184, 200
feminine 170, 183, 184, 185
fertility 90, 197, 202
field 47, 55, 63, 83, 135, 144, 145, 146, 152, 159, 163, 195
fight 42, 43, 150, 173, 177
fighting their symptoms 42
fight or flight 173
financial 25, 31, 41, 81, 99, 114, 128, 136, 166, 178, 182
First Nations 14, 17, 22
First Peoples 12, 17, 18, 21, 26, 27
fit into their family 129, 160, 188
flashbacks 159
flight 173
forgotten 27, 28, 36, 46, 51, 89, 136, 162, 187
former significant partners 9, 46
fostering 60, 80, 97, 129

O

obligation 126
obstacles 4, 119, 188
off balance 115
old habits 2, 68
old institutions 2
old neuronal pathways 2
old pattern of behaviour 2
old thought patterns 2
organization 2, 16
organize 98, 109
orphans 46, 82
ovaries 116, 184
overcompensate 117, 118
overhaul yourself emotionally 181

P

pain 17, 23, 26, 27, 43, 52, 56, 62, 89, 101, 165, 174, 181, 185
paralysis 26
parenting 17, 23, 85, 117, 201
parents v, 14, 16, 18, 19, 24, 39, 42, 45, 46, 48, 52, 55, 57, 60, 62, 63, 70, 76, 79, 83, 84, 85, 86, 87, 88, 91, 94, 103, 106, 115, 117, 122, 123, 124, 125, 126, 127, 128, 133, 134, 138, 141, 144, 146, 147, 148, 150, 152, 160, 161, 162, 166, 168, 169, 170, 174, 178, 179, 181, 200, 201, 203
partner gets close 117
partners 51, 71, 76, 81, 82, 83, 85, 86, 87, 90, 93, 106, 116, 117, 119, 124, 125, 128, 132, 143, 157, 158, 159, 170, 181
patriarchy 5, 138, 140, 141, 142, 143, 144, 147, 148, 151, 153, 155, 187
patterns 10, 15, 26, 57, 61, 62, 68, 80, 98, 99, 106, 111, 112, 118, 122, 123, 127, 135, 159, 160, 167, 176, 179, 180, 202
Payne, John L. vi, 196
peace iv, 53, 64, 188, 192, 195
peaceful possibilities iv, 188, 192
perception 51, 56, 98, 103, 122, 136, 147, 148, 160, 163, 167, 182, 198
perpetrator 9, 14, 25, 33, 46, 67, 87, 150, 160, 163, 164, 165, 166, 194, 197
personal wounds 13
personal wounds of colonization 13
phenomena 139
phenomenological 6, 39, 55, 81, 139, 150, 191
physical 1, 3, 4, 8, 18, 23, 25, 31, 38, 41, 50, 55, 59, 60, 66, 70, 83, 84, 85, 87, 92, 95, 98, 99, 102, 103, 105, 107, 108, 112, 114, 116, 119, 124, 128, 130, 136, 159, 166, 181
political 2, 21, 81
power 3, 16, 27, 42, 141, 145, 147, 151, 162, 169, 177, 185, 192, 197, 201, 203
pregnancy 50, 79, 80, 85, 86, 100, 102, 116, 132, 142, 191